SPACE
IN 30 SECONDS

First published in the UK in 2013 by

Ivy Press

210 High Street

Lewes

East Sussex BN7 2NS

United Kingdom

www.ivypress.co.uk

ISBN: 978-1-908005-73-1

This book was conceived, designed and produced by

Ivy Press

CREATIVE DIRECTOR Peter Bridgewater

MANAGING EDITOR Hazel Songhurst

PROJECT EDITOR Cath Senker

ART DIRECTOR Kevin Knight

DESIGNER Jane Hawkins and Lisa McCormick

ILLUSTRATORS

Melvyn Evans (colour)

Marta Munoz (black and white)

Printed in China

Colour origination by Ivy Press Reprographics

10 9 8 7 6 5 4 3 2 1

SPACE
IN 30 SECONDS

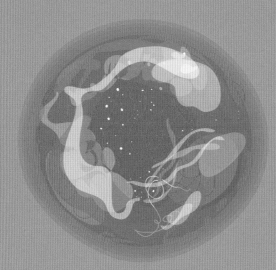

CLIVE GIFFORD

CONSULTANT: DR MIKE GOLDSMITH

Ivy Kids

Contents

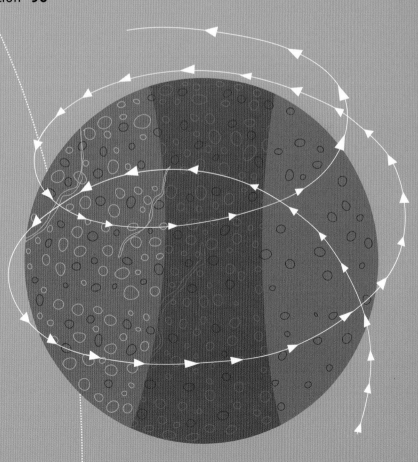

Space: what's out there?

...in 60 seconds

When we talk about space, we are talking about the Universe. The Universe is everything we can touch, feel, sense, measure or detect.
It includes living things, planets, stars, clouds of dust and the space in between all of these objects.

Space is so incredibly vast that it is impossible for humans to explore it directly. Yet over the past 100 years, astronomers and scientists have made huge advances in their understanding of space. To make their discoveries, they use scientific instruments to gather information about distant bodies such as stars or black holes.

To find out about planets, moons and other bodies nearer to the Earth, machines called probes are sent into space on missions of exploration. In August 2012, for example, a car-sized robot called the Curiosity Rover reached the surface of the planet Mars after a 563-million-km (350-million-mile) journey from Earth. It is going to spend at least two years exploring Earth's planetary neighbour, sending back information and photographs to Earth via radio waves.

This book looks at many important topics about space. It is divided into chapters on how the Universe began and might end, stars and their different types, the Sun and planets that make up the Solar System, galaxies, and how humans learn about space.

Every topic has a page you can read in 30 seconds to grasp the main facts – fast. If you're in a hurry, there is a 3-second sum-up to give you the basic idea in a nutshell. And the 3-minute missions give you the chance to discover some of the principles of space for yourself, from the comfort of your home on Earth.

The Big Bang

For centuries, humans have looked to the night sky and wondered how the Universe began, what shape it is and how big it might be. Many different theories have been put forward about the start of the Universe. At the present time, most cosmologists – space scientists – agree with a theory called the Big Bang. Far less certain is how the Universe might end in the distant future.

The Big Bang
Glossary

astronomer A scientist who studies the Sun, Moon, stars, planets and space in general.

atom The smallest part of an **element** that can take part in a chemical change.

Big Bang The sudden expansion that many scientists suggest created the **Universe**.

Big Chill One theory about how the **Universe** might end, with all the stars fading away and dying.

Big Crunch A theory about how the **Universe** might end, by collapsing into one dense point.

Big Rip The theory that the **Universe** could end by everything in it being ripped apart.

dark energy A kind of energy that scientists believe may make up more than 70 per cent of the **Universe** but they do not know exactly what it is.

dense Heavy in relation to its size, so that a tiny amount is extremely heavy.

element A simple chemical substance that is made up of **atoms** of only one type. It cannot be split into a simpler substance.

expansion The act of something getting bigger.

galaxy A grouping of stars, dust and gas clouds that may also contain planets. Our galaxy is the Milky Way, which contains our Sun and its planets as well as many other stars. All the stars we can see without a telescope belong to the Milky Way.

gravity A force that pulls objects in space towards each other. Around Earth, it pulls them towards the planet, so things fall to the ground when you drop them.

light year The distance that light travels in one year.

Local Group The collection of galaxies that our **galaxy** is part of.

mass The quantity of material that something contains.

matter All the substances and objects in the **Universe** that have **mass** and take up space.

nucleus The central part of an **atom** that contains most of its **mass**.

Solar System The Sun and all the planets and other objects that move around it.

telescope A scientific instrument that gathers in light or other signals from space to allow people to study distant objects.

Universe The whole of space and everything in it, including the Earth, the planets and the stars.

The Universe begins

...in 30 seconds

The Universe is everything that exists. It's phenomenally huge. Imagine something as big as you can, multiply it by a billion and you're still nowhere near how big it is!

Scientists who study the Universe believe in a theory called the Big Bang to explain how the Universe was formed.

The Big Bang wasn't an explosion. It was an unbelievably sudden expansion out of a single point. Everything expanded out of this single point including space, energy and matter – all the physical things in the Universe. Forces such as gravity formed. Time was created. There is no 'before' the Big Bang. It's hard to get your head around!

Within 3 seconds of the Big Bang, the three simplest elements had formed: hydrogen, helium and lithium.

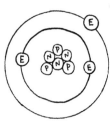

The earliest stars formed between 50 and 150 million years later, followed by galaxies. Around 9 billion years after the Big Bang, the Solar System and Earth were created.

3-second sum-up

The Universe probably began with the Big Bang.

How old is the Universe?

It's 13,700 million years old! Imagine its history squeezed into a year on Earth.

- The Big Bang was within the first second of 1 January.

- The Earth formed in September and the first dinosaurs appeared on 24 December.

- Humans appeared late evening on 31 December. The Ancient Romans arrived 4 seconds before midnight.

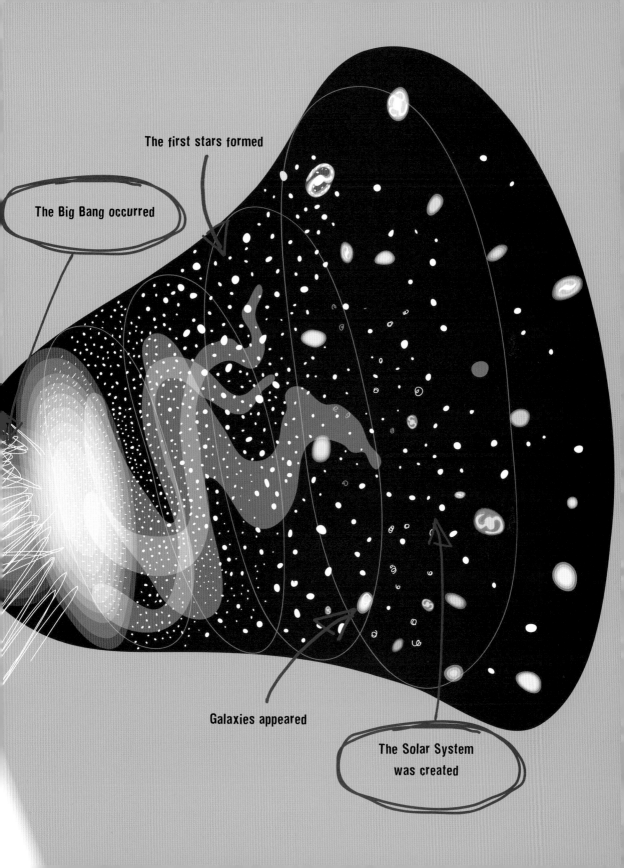

The expanding Universe

...in 30 seconds

Ever since the Big Bang, the Universe has been expanding and still is to this day. How did scientists find out?

In 1929, astronomer Edwin Hubble observed galaxies using the world's biggest telescope at the time. He was able to measure how groups of galaxies were moving away from other groups of galaxies.

Think of the groups of galaxies as raisins in bread dough. As the dough rises, the raisins move further apart from each other. So, distant clusters of galaxies are moving away from our Local Group of galaxies. And the further they are, the faster they go.

In the 1990s, scientists found that space wasn't expanding at one set speed, but that the expansion was accelerating (speeding up). Many scientists believe that this is caused by dark energy – a mysterious energy that makes up more than 70 per cent of the Universe.

3-second sum-up

The Universe is expanding fast!

3-minute mission Make an expanding Universe

1 Slightly inflate a large balloon and clip a peg over the end to keep in the air.

2 Mark ten swirls with a marker pen on the balloon. Each swirl is a cluster of galaxies. Mark a tiny M for the Milky Way.

3 Inflate the balloon to about two-thirds full size and see how the distances increase between the swirls.

4 Fully inflate the balloon to see the distances increase again. The swirls are not moving on the balloon. It is the balloon that is getting bigger, just like space is expanding.

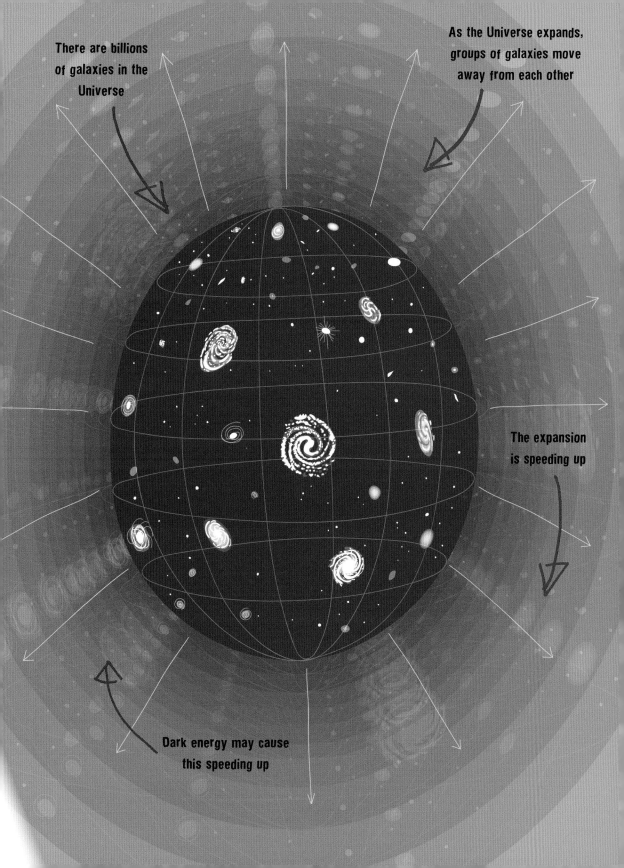

Light years

...in 30 seconds

A light year is a unit of measurement to describe how far away objects are in space. Light moves incredibly quickly, covering 299,792 km (186,282 miles) a second, and an unbelievable 9,460,730,472,580 km – about 9.4 trillion km – in a year.

So one light year is about 9.4 trillion km (6 trillion miles).

Why do we need to use light years? Well, the Universe is HUGE and distances between objects are so big that using miles or kilometers just isn't useful.

The nearest galaxy, Andromeda, is a whopping 21,000,000,000,000,000,000 km away – 21 quintillion km, or 13,000,000,000,000,000,000 miles. Just look at all those figures!

These numbers have so many figures, it's hard to work out what they mean. So astronomers use light years instead, and would say that Andromeda is 2,300,000 light years (2.3 million light years) away.

3-second sum-up

Nothing can travel faster than the speed of light.

3-minute mission Work out a You Year

A YOU YEAR is how far YOU would travel running 24 hours a day, 365 days a year, at full speed.

1 Time how many seconds it takes to run 100 metres.

2 Divide 100 by your time to see how many metres you travel in 1 second.

3 Multiply this by 60, then 60, then 24, then 365.

4 Divide the answer by 1,000 to get the distance in kilometres you would travel in a year – a YOU YEAR.

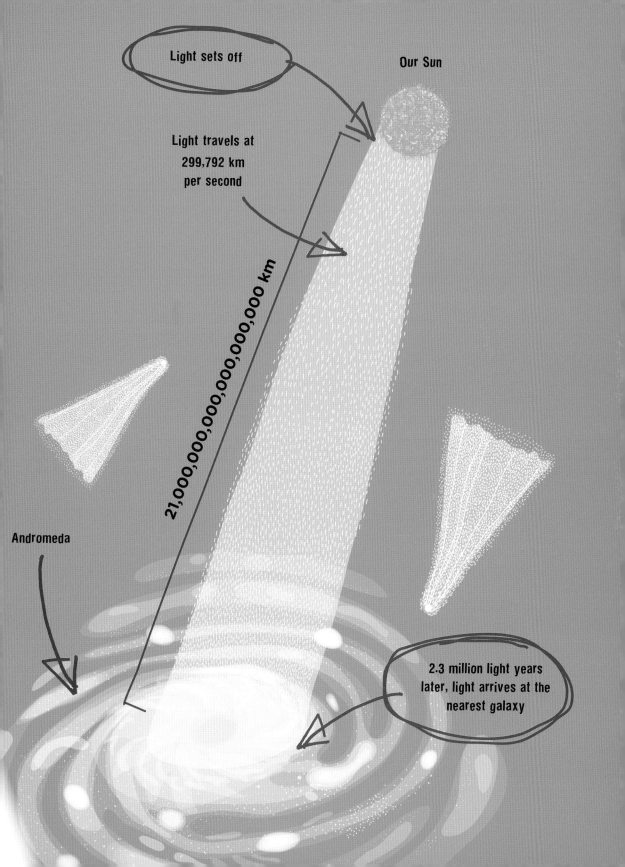

Crunch time

...in 30 seconds

Will the Universe end? No one actually knows. If the Universe continues to expand, a Big Chill could happen. Galaxies would become further and further apart and eventually run out of gas to make new stars.

The existing stars would run out of fuel and slowly fade away. The Universe would dim and cool until it became very cold and dark.

Another more violent ending is the Big Rip. In this theory, space continues to expand in the Universe, but this expansion starts to occur within galaxies, causing them to separate, then in stars, pulling them apart. It would continue in planets and finally, individual atoms. Everything would be 'ripped' apart by the expansion.

This all sounds awful, but relax! No scientist is predicting the end of the Universe anytime soon. Any ending is billions of years away.

3-second sum-up

The Universe might end by freezing, ripping apart or collapsing completely.

The Big Crunch

In the past, one popular theory for the end of the Universe was the Big Crunch.

The idea was that the Universe could only expand a certain amount before the force of gravity started to pull it back, just like an elastic band.

Everything in the Universe would become closer and closer until the Universe collapsed into one extremely dense point.

18

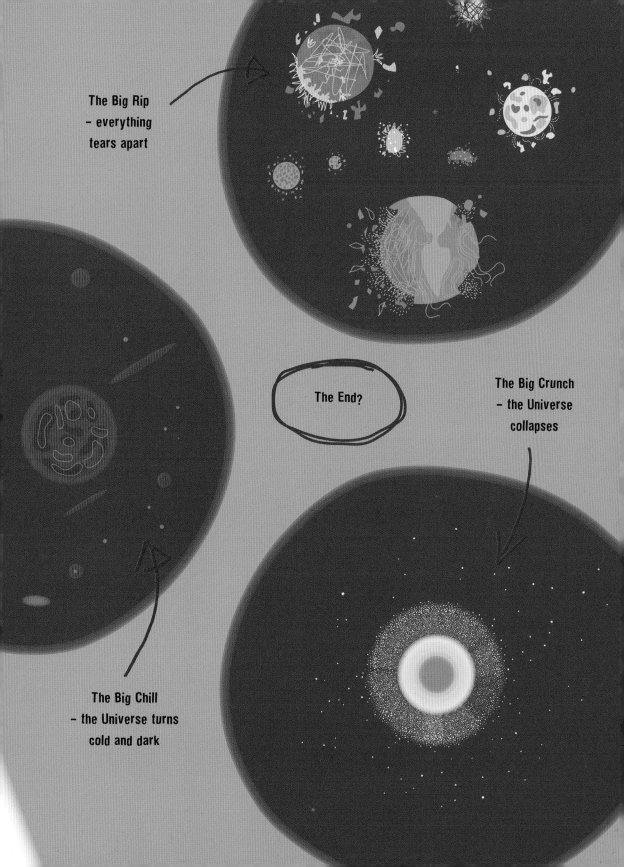

The Big Rip
– everything
tears apart

The End?

The Big Crunch
– the Universe
collapses

The Big Chill
– the Universe turns
cold and dark

Stars

Stars are giant balls of gas that burn fiercely. The smallest may be a tenth of the size of our Sun. The largest may be more than 100 times bigger! We can see thousands of stars in the night sky from Earth. But they are just a tiny fraction of the total number in the Universe – scientists believe there are billions of billions of them.

Glossary

apparent magnitude How bright a star looks from Earth.

astronomer A scientist who studies the Sun, Moon, stars, planets and space in general.

atom The smallest part of an element (a simple chemical substance) that can take part in a chemical change.

constellation A group of stars that forms a shape in the sky and has a name.

dense Heavy in relation to its size, so that a tiny amount is extremely heavy.

diameter A straight line from one side of a circle across the middle to the other side.

galaxy A grouping of stars, dust and gas clouds that may also have planets. Our galaxy is the Milky Way, which contains our Sun and its planets as well as many other stars. All the stars we can see without a telescope belong to the Milky Way.

gravity A force that pulls objects in space towards each other. Around Earth, it pulls them towards the planet, so things fall to the ground when you drop them.

light year The distance that light travels in one year.

mass The quantity of material that something contains.

matter All the substances and objects in the **Universe** that have **mass** and take up space.

nebula (plural nebulae) A huge cloud of dust and gas. Some nebulae form stars.

neutron A very small piece of **matter** that forms part of the **nucleus** of an **atom**.

neutron star A type of extremely dense star.

nuclear fusion When the **nuclei** of **atoms** are fused together (combined) to form a larger **nucleus**, and energy is released.

nuclear reaction When the nuclei of **atoms** are changed from one element into another.

nucleus (plural nuclei) The central part of an **atom** that contains most of its **mass**.

orbit A curved path followed by a planet (or an object) as it moves around a planet or a star. To orbit is to go around another planet or star.

Orion nebula One of the closest **nebulae** to Earth.

planetary nebula When some stars die, a cloud called a planetary **nebula** is formed. The core then forms a **white dwarf** and eventually the star fades away.

pressure The force or weight with which something presses against something else.

protostar A clump of matter (substance) that forms as part of the birth of a star.

red dwarf A small star that is not very hot.

red giant A large star towards the end of its life that is quite cool for a star and gives out a reddish light.

Solar System The Sun and all the planets and other objects that move around it.

supernova, Type II (plural supernovae) A star that suddenly becomes much brighter and gives out a huge amount of energy because it is exploding and will die.

Universe The whole of space and everything in it, including the Earth, the planets and the stars.

white dwarf A small star that has died and is very **dense**.

Star birth

...in 30 seconds

Some nebulae form stars. Nebulae are gigantic clouds of dust and gas found throughout the Universe.

The Orion nebula is one of the closest to Earth, about 1,340 light years away. It's over 24 light years wide, that's – wait for it – more than 227,000,000,000,000 km (141,000,000,000,000 miles)!

A local supernova (star explosion) or another star passing close by can trigger parts of the cloud to start to contract under the force of its own gravity. As the parts become smaller and draw in more dust and gas, they become denser and hotter and form a clump of matter called a protostar.

The core starts to collapse in on itself, increasing in pressure and temperature, and causing nuclear fusion. This fuses hydrogen atoms together into helium atoms and produces huge amounts of energy. Out of the protostar, a star forms.

3-second sum-up

Stars are born in giant star nurseries called nebulae.

3-minute mission Go star spotting

Constellations are patterns of stars we can see in the night sky. They change their positions throughout the year. Print or copy out a star map from a book or website. On a clear night, try to spot three constellations.

http://www.kidsastronomy.com/astroskymap/constellations.htm

http://www.astronomynow.com/sky_chart.shtml

http://downloads.bbc.co.uk/tv/guides/bbc_stargazing_live_star_guide.pdf

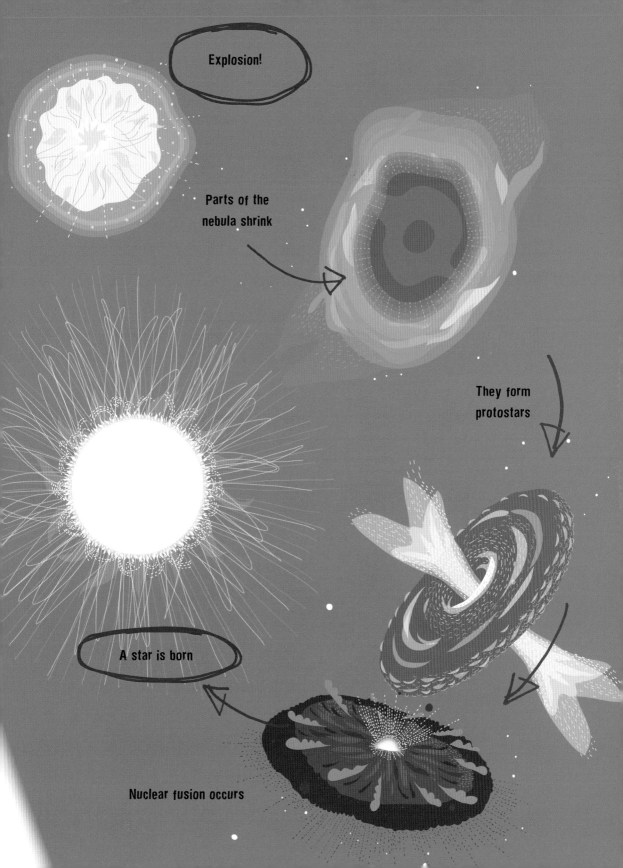

Types of stars

...in 30 seconds

Stars vary in size, temperature and how bright they appear from Earth.

The Sun is a pretty average-sized star. Some are smaller; others are far larger. Betelgeuse (betel-jooz), in the Orion constellation, is a gigantic star. If Betelgeuse replaced our Sun, its outer surface would extend out as far as the orbit of Jupiter!

Other stars are even larger. VY Canis Majoris, in the constellation Canis Major, is the largest known star. Scientists believe it is 3,000 million km (1,900 million miles) in diameter – more than 2,000 times the diameter of the Sun.

Stars burn at different temperatures. Astronomers group stars into classes called spectral types, depending on how hot they are. Type 0 is the hottest, with surface temperatures of over 30,000°C. That's hot! Only around one in 3 million stars are Type 0 and they tend to shine extremely brightly. Lying some 5,000 light years from us, the Type 0 star Cygnus OB2-12 is 6 million times brighter than our Sun.

3-second sum-up

Some stars are bigger, brighter and hotter than others.

How bright do they shine?

Stars can also be classified by how brightly they appear to shine to us as we view them from Earth. This classification is called 'apparent magnitude'.

The Sun is, of course, the brightest star, followed by Sirius, the brightest in the night sky, then Canopus and Arcturus.

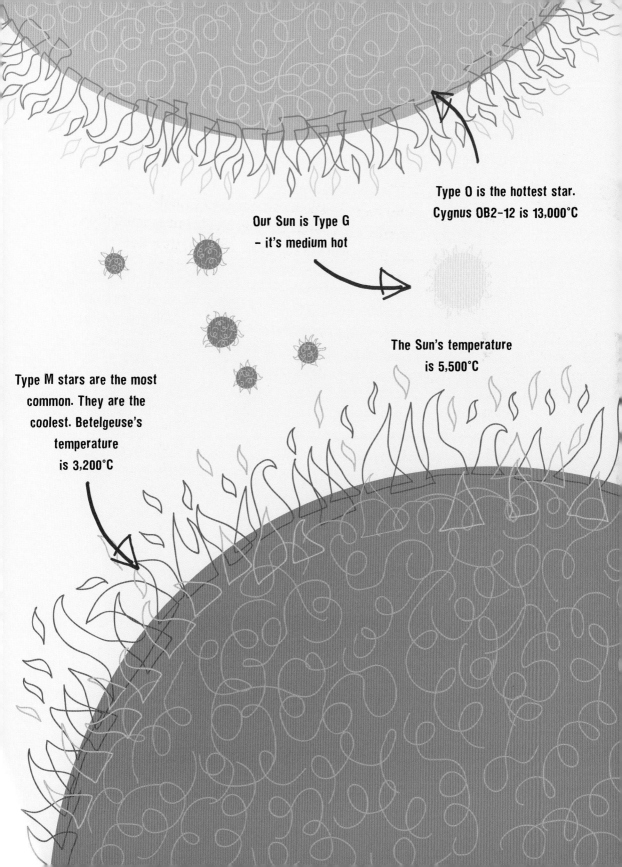

Type O is the hottest star.
Cygnus OB2-12 is 13,000°C

Our Sun is Type G
– it's medium hot

The Sun's temperature
is 5,500°C

Type M stars are the most
common. They are the
coolest. Betelgeuse's
temperature
is 3,200°C

Supernovae
...in 30 seconds

Stars die in different ways. One of the most spectacular ways is a Type II supernova. This occurs when a massive star no longer has enough fuel to keep nuclear fusion occurring at its core (centre). The core collapses sharply under the force of gravity and incredible temperatures are generated – as high as 100 billion°C!

The core of the supernova rebounds, sending matter hurtling out into space as fast as 15,000 to 40,000 km (9,000 to 25,000 miles) per second. In one second, a supernova can generate as much energy as a small star does in its lifetime. Some supernovae continue to shine 10 billion times as brightly as a normal star for months.

Supernovae are quite rare events to spot, but keep your eyes peeled when stargazing and you never know. In 2011, Kathryn Aurora Gray, a 10-year-old Canadian schoolgirl, became the youngest person ever to discover a new supernova, occurring 240 million light years away in a galaxy called UGC3378.

3-second sum-up

A Type II supernova is a giant explosion that rips a star apart.

3-minute mission The supernova effect

See how energy from the rebounding core of a supernova forces away the outer layers of a star:

1 Drop a basketball (or football) and a tennis ball on hard ground one at a time, noting how far they bounce.

2 Next, hold the tennis ball (outer layers of a star) on top of the basketball (star's core). Drop them together.

3 The tennis ball will fly away with great force, just as the outer layers of a star are blown away by the core in a supernova.

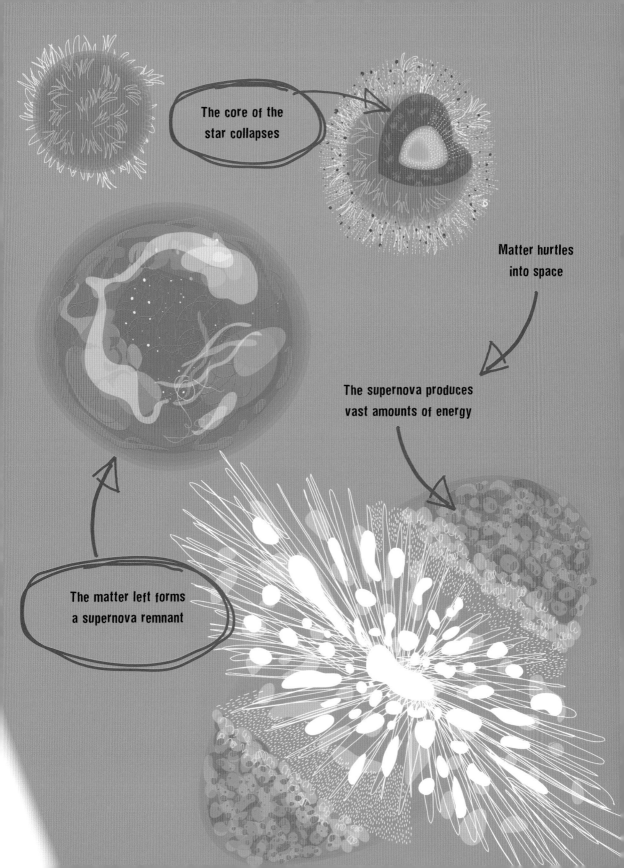

The core of the
star collapses

Matter hurtles
into space

The supernova produces
vast amounts of energy

The matter left forms
a supernova remnant

Quiet star death

...in 30 seconds

Stars don't all end in spectacular supernovae. Red dwarfs are stars with less than half of the Sun's mass but that still have nuclear reactions in their core. These stars have quiet endings, gradually shrinking and growing dim as they run out of fuel.

Stars between half and eight times the mass of the Sun have more complex endings.

As they exhaust their hydrogen fuel at their centre, they start using helium as fuel and swell in size, becoming red giants. Eventually they cast off their outer shell or layers, to form a cloud called a planetary nebula. The core is called a white dwarf.

White dwarfs are small, extremely dense stars mostly made of carbon. A typical white dwarf is around the same size or slightly bigger than Earth but contains as much matter as the Sun. A white dwarf will slowly cool and fade over many billions of years.

3-second sum-up

Some stars shrink and die out while others swell then cool.

Neutron stars

White dwarfs are dense, but neutron stars are even denser. Neutron stars are formed from a supernova that leaves an unbelievably dense core of neutrons.

A teaspoon of neutron star might weigh more than 1 million tonnes. A neutron star may be less than 20 km (12 miles) in diameter but contain as much matter as the entire Solar System!

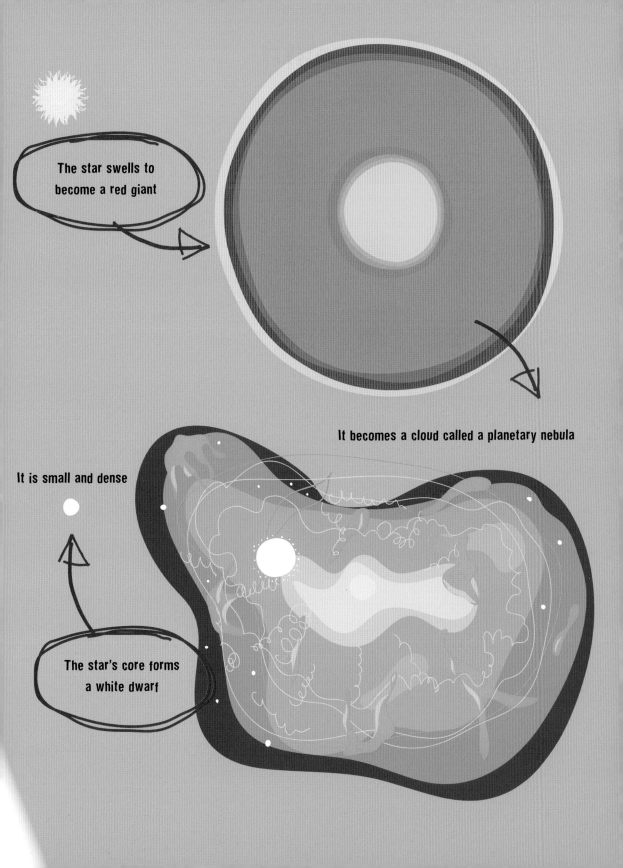

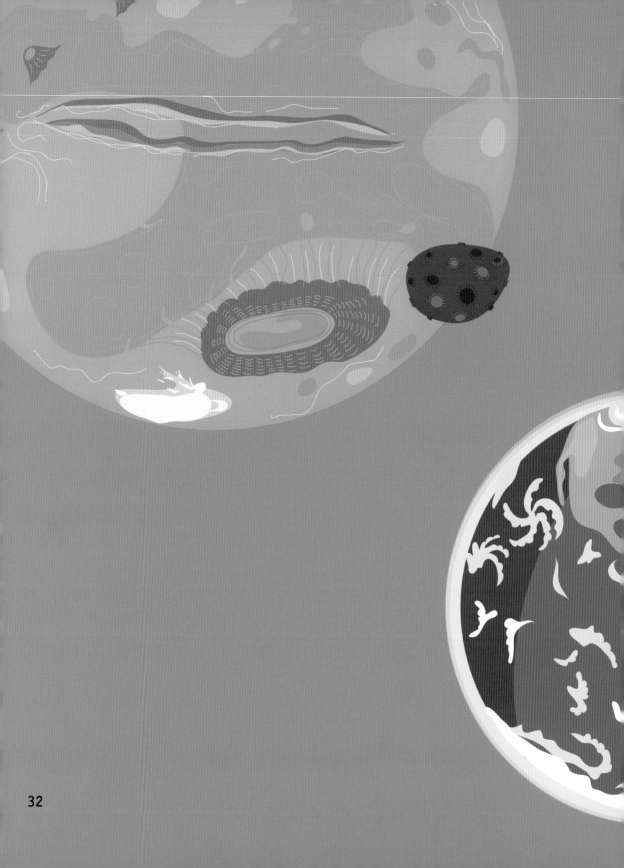

Sun and inner planets

The Sun is an average-sized star moving
through space. The pull of its gravity keeps eight
planets, their moons and other bodies travelling
around it along elliptical (oval) paths called orbits.
The four planets closest to the Sun are Mercury,
Venus, Earth and Mars. They are called the
terrestrial planets because they have solid, rocky
surfaces. These, along with the Sun, asteroids,
comets, dust, gas, meteoroids and a dwarf
planet make up the inner Solar System.

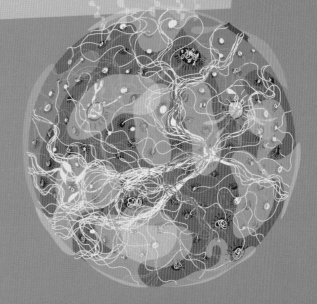

Glossary

asteroid A small body of rock, metal or both that **orbits** the Sun.

astronomer A scientist who studies the Sun, Moon, stars, planets and space in general.

astronomical unit (AU) A unit of distance. 1 AU equals 149.6 million km (93 million miles), roughly the distance between the middle of the Earth and the middle of the Sun.

atmosphere The mixture of gases that surrounds a planet.

atom The smallest part of an element (a simple chemical substance) that can take part in a chemical change.

axis An imaginary line through the middle of an object, such as a planet, around which the object turns.

canyon A deep valley with steep sides of rock.

chromosphere The Sun's inner **atmosphere**. Chromosphere means 'sphere of colour'.

convective zone An inner layer of the Sun, after the **radiative** layer.

corona The outer **atmosphere** of the Sun, which is bigger than the Sun itself.

crater A large hole in the ground often caused by something big hitting it from space, such as an **asteroid**.

diameter A straight line from one side of a circle across the centre to the other side.

dwarf planet A large object in space, such as Pluto, that goes around the Sun but is not as large as a planet.

gravity A force that pulls objects in space towards each other. Around Earth, it pulls them towards the planet, so things fall to the ground when you drop them.

km/h Kilometres per hour; a measure of speed.

maria The rocky plains on the Moon.

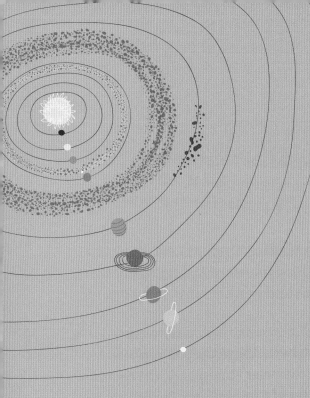

mass The quantity of material that something contains.

nuclear reaction When the nuclei of **atoms** are changed from one element (simple chemical substance) into another.

orbit A curved path followed by a planet (or an object) as it moves around a planet or a star. To orbit is to go around another planet or star.

photosphere The surface of the Sun that you can see.

polar ice cap A layer of ice permanently covering parts of the Earth, and Mars, around the North and South Poles.

pressure The force or weight with which something presses against something else.

radiative layer The part of the Sun next to the core. Heat from the core is transferred through the radiative layer outwards.

rotation The action of an object moving in a circle around a central point, for example, the Earth spinning on its **axis**.

Solar System The Sun and all the planets and other objects that move around it.

space probe A spacecraft without people on board that obtains information and sends it back to Earth.

telescope A scientific instrument that gathers in light or other signals from space to allow people to study distant objects.

volcanic lava Hot, liquid rock that comes out of a volcano.

The Sun

...in 30 seconds

The Sun is the star at the heart of the Solar System. Its great mass creates the gravity that keeps planets, asteroids and other bodies orbiting around it. It provides heat and light.

In its core, the Sun is a giant nuclear furnace. Every second, there are nuclear reactions. More than 600 million tonnes of hydrogen atoms are fused together to create helium atoms and vast amounts of energy.

This energy travels through the Sun's radiative and convective layers to its surface – the photosphere. Above the photosphere lies the chromosphere and then the outer atmosphere, the corona. The corona can reach temperatures of 1 to 2 million °C. HOT!

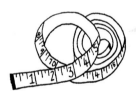

3-second sum-up

The Sun gives heat and light to our Solar System.

3-minute mission Measure the Sun

Measure the Sun with a piece of card, a pin, white paper and ruler.
Remember: Never look directly at the Sun!

1   Make a pinhole in the middle of the card and hold it so that sunlight shines through the hole onto the white paper. Try to get as much distance as possible between the card and paper to create a bigger image (1 m/3 ft or more is ideal).

2   Get a friend to measure the diameter of the image on the paper and the distance from the pinhole to the paper. Add these figures to the maths equation below.

$$\frac{\text{Diameter of Sun on paper}}{\text{Distance from pinhole to paper}} \times 149,600,00 \text{ km (Earth to Sun distance)} = \text{Diameter of Sun in km}$$

How close were you to the Sun's real size?

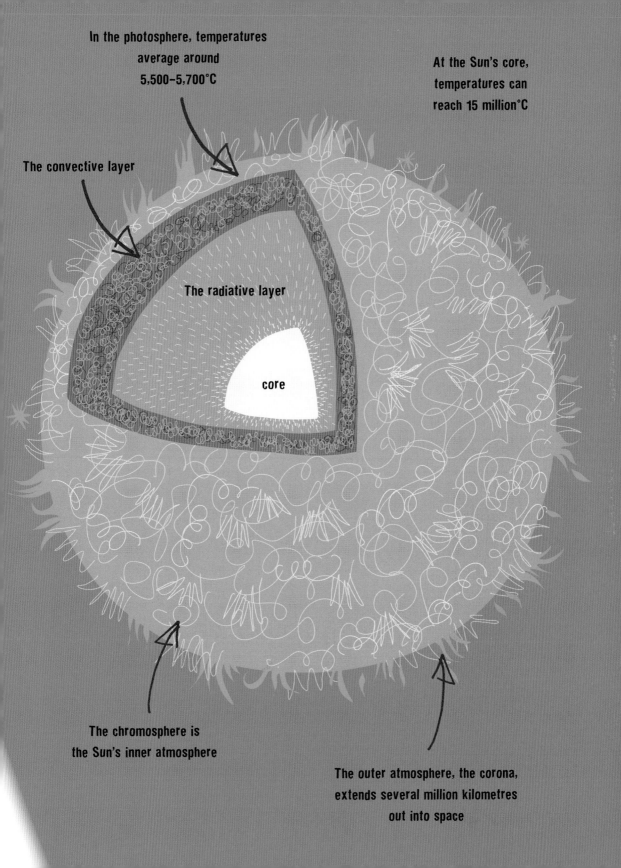

In the photosphere, temperatures average around 5,500–5,700°C

At the Sun's core, temperatures can reach 15 million°C

The convective layer

The radiative layer

core

The chromosphere is the Sun's inner atmosphere

The outer atmosphere, the corona, extends several million kilometres out into space

Mercury

...in 30 seconds

Mercury is the closest planet to the Sun. On average, it is 57.9 million km (36 million miles) from the Sun. Mercury is the smallest planet in our Solar System.

Mercury's orbit around the Sun takes just 88 Earth days to complete so its year is a quarter of the length of Earth's.

All planets spin on their axis and a complete rotation is known as a day. A day on Earth lasts almost 24 hours, but on Mercury, which spins very slowly, a full rotation takes more than 1,400 hours to complete – that's over 58 days on Earth. So there are less than two Mercury days to its year.

Temperatures on Mercury can reach as high as 427°C when the Sun strikes directly. Out of the Sun's rays, they can plummet to below -170°C.

Large parts of the planet's surface are covered in craters of various sizes. Astronomers believe that Mercury was bombarded by asteroids during the early stages of the Solar System's formation.

3-second sum-up

Tiny Mercury can be baking hot or freezing cold.

3-minute mission Make craters!

Mix flour and a little water in a mixing bowl to form a soft but not runny mixture. Fill a large tray or casserole dish with the mixture and take it outside.

Standing directly above the bowl, drop different-sized round objects (such as a marble and a golf ball) into the tray from knee, chest and above-head height. Note the different-sized craters formed by different objects impacting on the surface at different speeds.

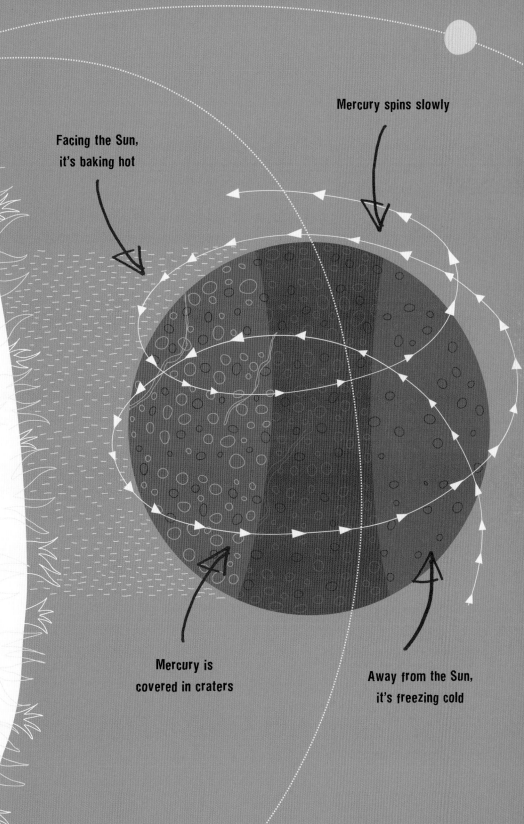

Mercury spins slowly

Facing the Sun,
it's baking hot

Mercury is
covered in craters

Away from the Sun,
it's freezing cold

Venus

...in 30 seconds

Venus is the second closest planet to the Sun and is a similar size to Earth. It's the hottest planet in the Solar System.

Venus takes 224.7 Earth days to complete an orbit around the Sun, which is quite quick. But when it comes to turning on its own axis, Venus is a serious slowcoach. It takes a staggering 243 Earth days to complete a rotation. Its day is longer than its year!

Venus has an average surface temperature of approximately 462°C – that's more than enough to melt the metal lead.

There's little let-up either, because its atmosphere acts like a really thick blanket, keeping in all that heat. Venus' atmosphere is around 96 per cent carbon dioxide, 3.5 per cent nitrogen, some sulphur and almost no oxygen or water vapour – substances needed for animal life.

The thick atmosphere presses down on the surface with 90 times more pressure than Earth's atmosphere. Even if you survived a descent through the poisonous clouds of gases, the pressure on the surface of Venus would squash you flat.

3-second sum-up

Venus is extremely hot with a poisonous atmosphere.

Visiting Venus

The thick, toxic atmosphere makes it difficult for astronomers to view the surface of Venus from Earth, but space probes such as Magellan, Venus Express and the Venera series of probes have reached and studied Venus using instruments that scan through the clouds.

They found a lifeless surface littered with volcanoes, some craters and plains made of volcanic lava.

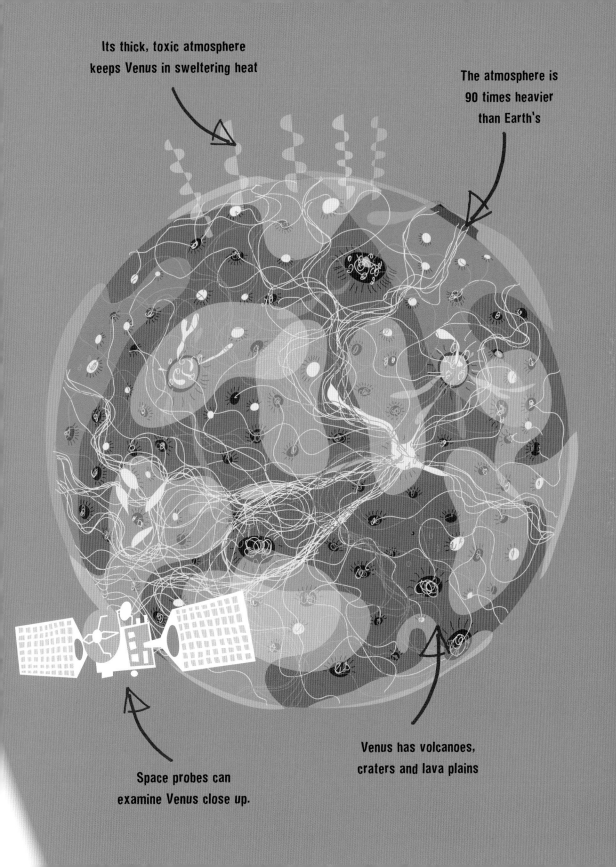

Its thick, toxic atmosphere
keeps Venus in sweltering heat

The atmosphere is
90 times heavier
than Earth's

Space probes can
examine Venus close up.

Venus has volcanoes,
craters and lava plains

Earth and Moon

...in 30 seconds

Earth lies an average of 149,597,870.7 km (92,955,807 miles) from the Sun. That figure equals 1 astronomical unit (AU), a unit of measurement used in the Solar System. For example, Jupiter is around 5.2 AU from the Sun.

Our planet is seriously on the move, whizzing through space on its 939.9-million-km (584-million-mile) orbit round the Sun. As it orbits, Earth also turns on its own axis. It turns to face the Sun every 23 hours, 56 minutes and 4 seconds, giving us our day and night.

Earth is tilted at an angle of 23.5°. This tilt creates the seasons. The hemisphere (half) of the Earth tilted more to the Sun enjoys summer while the other half experiences winter. As Earth continues its orbit, the seasons change.

Surrounding the planet, and protecting it from many of the Sun's harmful rays, is the Earth's atmosphere. The atmosphere keeps Earth's surface warm and enables life to function.

Earth's one Moon is an average of 0.0026 AU (384,400 km/238,855 miles) away from Earth. It is marked with hundreds of craters and flattish rocky plains called maria.

3-second sum-up

You're standing on a body travelling at over 107,000 km/h (66,500 mph) around the Sun.

3-minute mission Make a Moon map

Get a set of binoculars or a telescope, pick a night with good, clear skies and make your own Moon map, sketching out any features you can see. Can you spot any craters or maria?

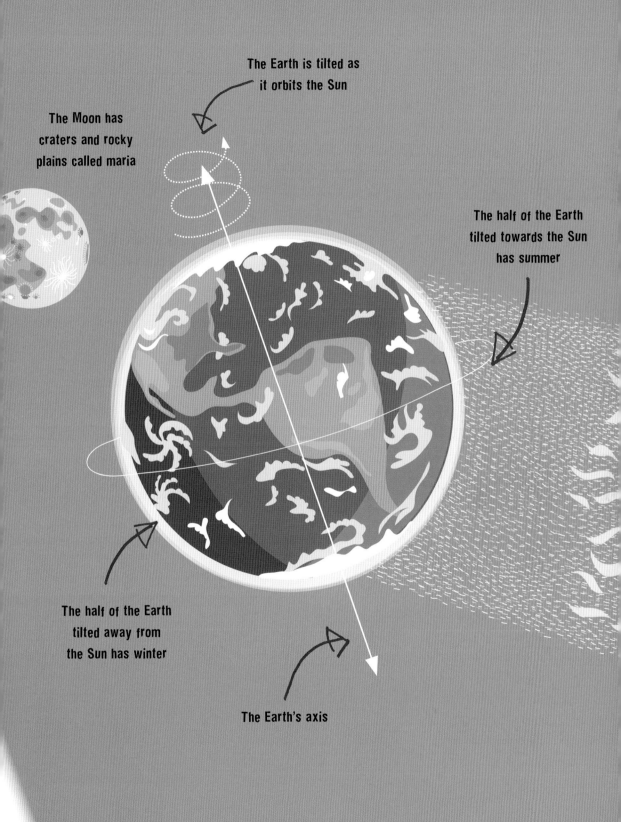

The Earth is tilted as it orbits the Sun

The Moon has craters and rocky plains called maria

The half of the Earth tilted towards the Sun has summer

The half of the Earth tilted away from the Sun has winter

The Earth's axis

Mars

...in 30 seconds

Mars is the second smallest planet in the Solar System – it's just over half the size of Earth. With no seas of liquid water on its surface, it has about as much land as our planet. Much of this looks like a rocky, dusty desert strewn with craters and plains.

Yet in places, Mars boasts some of the Solar System's most spectacular features: a gigantic canyon system called the Valles Marineris, a huge volcano and a massive crater.

In comparison to these giant features, Mars' two moons are puny. Deimos and Phobos are not round and are shaped rather like two large potatoes. Phobos, the larger moon, has an average diameter of 27 km (16 miles).

Scientists have discovered the features of Mars using telescopes and visiting space probes. They have found that Mars' atmosphere is very thin and over 95 per cent of it is carbon dioxide. The planet has polar ice caps, made mostly of frozen carbon dioxide. Scientists have found frozen water on Mars, too.

3-second sum-up

Our close neighbour, Mars, contains desert, ice, volcanoes and craters.

3-minute mission Journey to Mars

A manned mission to and from Mars with some meaningful time on the planet might take three or more years. What would such a mission be like for explorers?

Try to list some of the challenges you think would be involved in travelling for so long and list five personal items you would take with you on such a long journey. Remember that most of the room in the spacecraft will be packed with supplies for the journey.

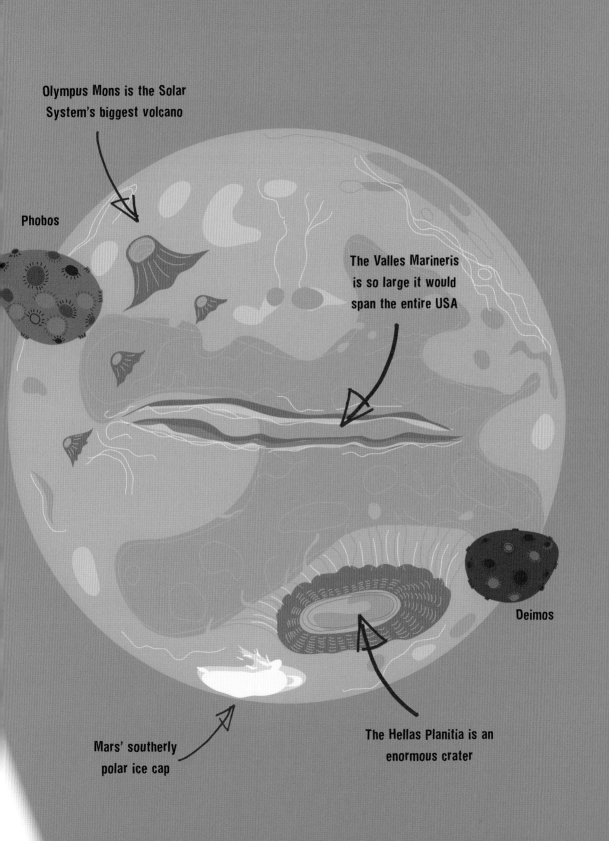

Olympus Mons is the Solar System's biggest volcano

Phobos

The Valles Marineris is so large it would span the entire USA

Deimos

Mars' southerly polar ice cap

The Hellas Planitia is an enormous crater

Asteroids and dwarf planets

...in 30 seconds

Asteroids are chunks of rock, metal or a mixture of both, which orbit the Sun. Many are found in the main belt – a giant, doughnut-shaped ring between Mars and Jupiter thought to contain more than a million asteroids bigger than 1 km (0.6 miles) in diameter.

These are believed to be leftovers from the Solar System's formation – chunks of material that never made it into a planet.

Asteroids are also found elsewhere in the Solar System. The Trojans are asteroids found along the path Jupiter takes as it orbits the Sun. There are also near-Earth asteroids, which are found inside Mars's orbit round the Sun.

When US astronomer Clyde Tombaugh discovered Pluto in 1930, it was classed as the ninth planet in the Solar System. In 2006, scientists reclassified Pluto as a dwarf planet. These are bodies that are basically round in shape, orbit the Sun but are not big enough to sweep all other material out of their path.

3-second sum-up

Asteroids are chunks of rock and metal. Dwarf planets are too small to be planets.

3-minute mission Space probe check

Two space probes, Dawn and New Horizons, are set to visit two dwarf planets in 2015. Visit the NASA space probe webpage at http://solarsystem.nasa.gov/missions

Click on the target button and select dwarf planets from the drop down menu. Check which ones are being visited and which other asteroid Dawn has already travelled to.

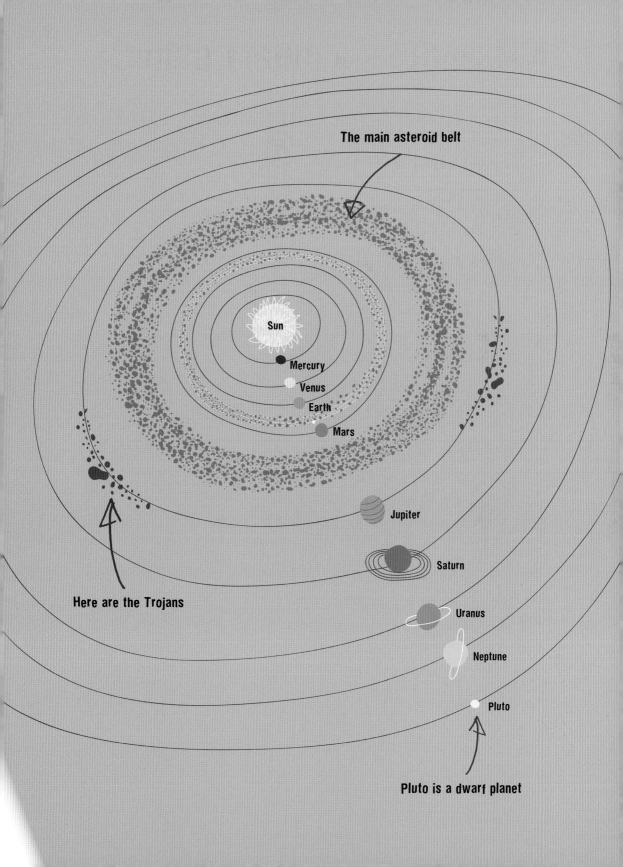

The main asteroid belt

Sun

Mercury

Venus

Earth

Mars

Jupiter

Saturn

Uranus

Neptune

Pluto

Here are the Trojans

Pluto is a dwarf planet

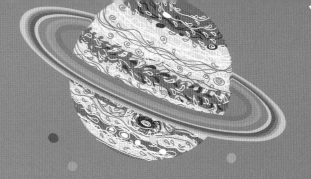

Outer solar system

Past Mars and the asteroid belt lies the outer Solar System. This vast region of space is home to the four gas giant planets – Jupiter, Saturn, Uranus and Neptune – and their many moons. Large numbers of comets are found here too. Beyond Neptune lie a number of small bodies including the Kuiper Belt objects and dwarf planets such as Pluto, Haumea and Eris. Far from the Sun, this region of the Solar System is freezing cold.

Glossary

astronomical unit (AU) A unit of distance. 1 AU equals 149.6 million km (93 million miles), roughly the distance between the middle of the Earth and the middle of the Sun.

atmosphere The mixture of gases that surround a planet.

axis An imaginary line through the middle of an object, such as a planet, around which the object turns.

coma The cloud of dust and gases around the core of a **comet**.

comet A mass of ice and dust that moves around the Sun.

dense Heavy in relation to its size, so that a tiny amount is extremely heavy.

diameter A straight line from one side of a circle across the centre to the other side.

element A simple chemical substance that is made up of atoms (the smallest parts of an element) of only one type. It cannot be split into a simpler substance.

equator An imaginary line around the middle of a planet at an equal distance from the North and South Poles. The poles are the two points at the opposite ends of the line on which a planet turns.

gravity A force that pulls objects in space towards each other. Around Earth, it pulls them towards the planet, so things fall to the ground when you drop them.

km/h Kilometres per hour; a measure of speed.

Kuiper Belt An area of the Solar System beyond Neptune, where **comets** are found.

mass The quantity of material that something contains.

mph Miles per hour; a measure of speed.

nucleus The central part of an atom (the smallest part of an element) that contains most of its mass.

Oort Cloud An area that scientists believe exists way beyond the **Kuiper Belt**, and where **comets** could be found.

orbit A curved path followed by a planet (or any object) as it moves around a planet or a star. To orbit is to go around another planet or star.

pole One of the two points at the opposite ends of the line on which a planet turns.

Solar System The Sun and all the planets and other objects that move around it.

space probe A spacecraft without people on board that obtains information and sends it back to Earth.

telescope A scientific instrument that gathers in light or other signals from space to allow people to study distant objects.

Jupiter

...in 30 seconds

Make no mistake about it, Jupiter is massive. The largest planet in the Solar System, Jupiter has a diameter of about 143,000 km (88,900 miles) across its equator. It is so large that all the other planets put together would total just 40 per cent of Jupiter's mass.

For its enormous size, Jupiter rotates about its own axis at seriously high speed, around 43,000 km/h (27,000 mph).

Jupiter is a gas giant, mostly made up of hydrogen and helium which many scientists think surrounds a small rocky core. As you get close to the centre, the gases turn to liquid.

Storms rage through the planet's atmosphere, and none come bigger than the Great Red Spot, a storm with 500 km/h (310 mph) winds, which has been observed for over 300 years. It varies in size but is currently around 20,000 km (12,000 miles) by 12,000 km (7,000 miles) – far bigger than Earth.

Jupiter's powerful gravity keeps over 60 moons in orbit around the planet.

3-second sum-up

Gigantic Jupiter is mostly made of gas.

3-minute mission Interplanetary weigh-in

Weight measures how strongly gravity pulls on objects. To find your weight on another planet, first weigh yourself on scales, then multiply your weight by the planet's gravity relative to Earth's gravity, listed below.

Mercury	0.38	Venus	0.91
Mars	0.38	Jupiter	2.54
Saturn	1.08	Uranus	0.91
Neptune	1.19	Pluto	0.06

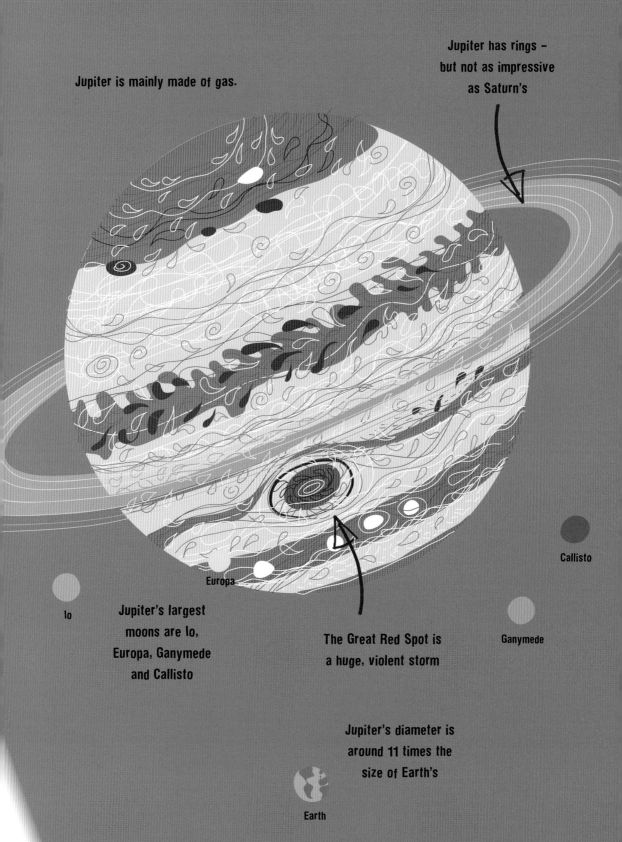

Saturn

...in 30 seconds

Saturn is the second largest planet in the Solar System. You could fit more than 760 Earth-sized objects inside Saturn! The planet is mostly made up of hydrogen and helium gas – two of the lightest elements in the Universe.

Saturn is the least dense of all the planets, only 70 per cent as dense as water. That means it would float in your bath, if your bath was big enough!

Jupiter, Uranus and Neptune all have rings but Saturn's are the biggest and most spectacular. Using space probes and scientific instruments, scientists have found they are made of billions of small rock, ice and dust particles held in place by Saturn's gravity.

3-second sum-up

Saturn is enormous but so light it could float in water!

3-minute mission Walk the Solar System

You'll need a large field and 9 balls. First, place a ball for the Sun. Measure a half-metre pace and work out how many paces to walk for each planet, using the guide below. Walk the Solar System as far as Saturn (and to Uranus and Neptune if you have room).

The scale you are using is 1 metre to every 20 million kilometres. The real Solar System is a staggering 20 billion times larger than your model!

Mercury	3 m	Venus	5.5 m	Earth	7.5 m
Mars	11.5 m	Jupiter	39 m	Saturn	71.5 m
Uranus	143.5 m	Neptune	225 m		

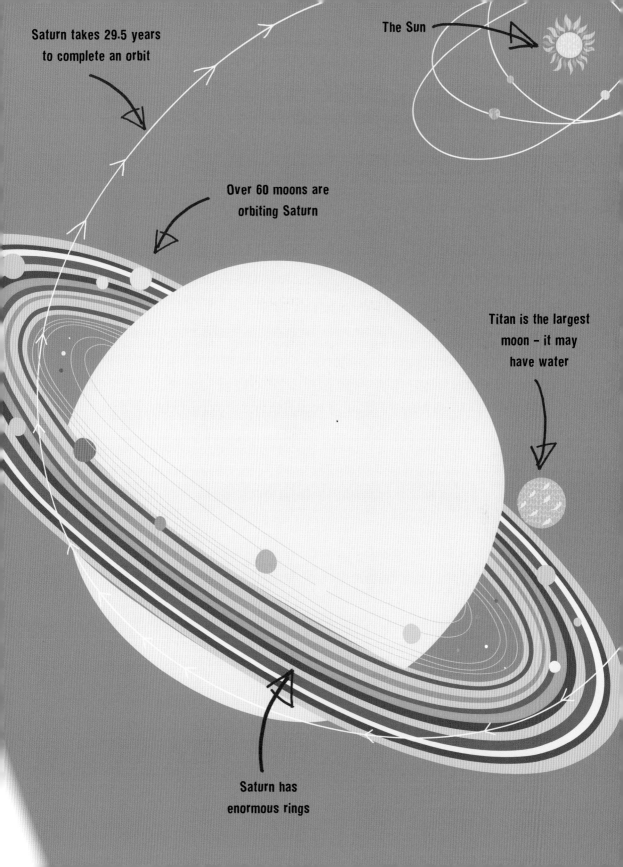

Saturn takes 29.5 years to complete an orbit

The Sun

Over 60 moons are orbiting Saturn

Titan is the largest moon – it may have water

Saturn has enormous rings

Uranus and Neptune

...in 30 seconds

Neptune is so far from the Sun that it takes sunlight more than 4 hours to reach Neptune. (It takes 8 minutes to reach Earth.) Uranus and Neptune receive a tiny fraction of the Sun's energy. As a result, they are extremely cold, with cloud surface temperatures dropping below -210°C. That's seriously cold!

Fierce storms rage across Neptune, driven by the most powerful winds found in the Solar System. Some have been measured travelling at 1,500 km/h (930 mph) – faster than a jet airliner on Earth.

Uranus takes 84.2 years to complete its journey round the Sun. Neptune takes a further 80 years to make a full orbit. So, you would have to be over 164 Earth years old to celebrate your first birthday on Neptune.

Uranus is tilted on its side, at an angle of 97.86°. At its poles, summer and winter last 42 years, until the planet has completed half of its orbit and the other half of Uranus faces the Sun.

3-second sum-up

Uranus and Neptune are bitterly cold planets with many moons.

Multiple moons

Uranus and Neptune have many moons. More have been discovered in recent years as telescopes have improved and space probes have visited the region.

At the latest count, Uranus has 27. Neptune has 13, including Triton, the coldest moon in the Solar System. Its surface is made of frozen nitrogen, carbon dioxide and water ice (ice made from water).

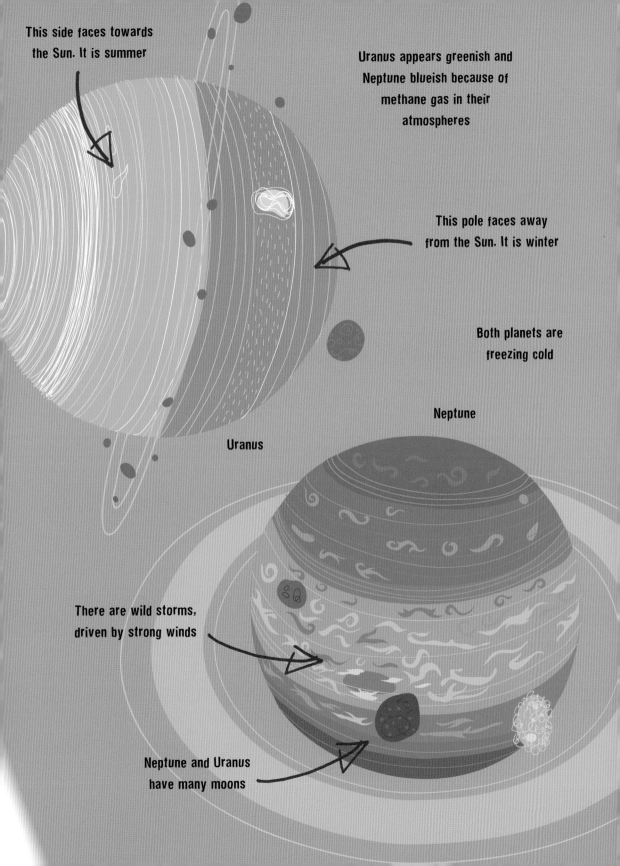

This side faces towards the Sun. It is summer

Uranus appears greenish and Neptune blueish because of methane gas in their atmospheres

This pole faces away from the Sun. It is winter

Both planets are freezing cold

Neptune

Uranus

There are wild storms, driven by strong winds

Neptune and Uranus have many moons

Comets

...in 30 seconds

You can imagine comets as dirty snowballs flying through space! They consist of ice and rock particles that form a solid nucleus, or core. Comets vary in size. The nucleus can be from a few hundred metres up to 40 km (25 miles) in diameter. These bodies orbit the Sun. For much of their journey, that's all there is to them.

Most comets are in the remotest parts of the Solar System. The Kuiper Belt is an area of the Solar System extending beyond Neptune for a further 25 AU (25 times the distance between Earth and the Sun). Way, way beyond Neptune and the Kuiper Belt may lie the Oort Cloud, some 50,000 AU away from the Sun.

A passing star may dislodge a comet, sending it towards the Sun. When a comet reaches around 6 AU from the Sun, warmth from the Sun heats up the nucleus. Some of the ice turns into gases, forming a large cloud around the nucleus called a coma, which can be 1,000 times bigger than the nucleus.

3-second sum-up

Comets are snowballs of ice and dust, hurtling around the Sun.

Comet's tails

Parts of the nucleus evaporate into gases while dust is dragged from the nucleus. Together they can form a long tail that always faces away from the Sun – or two tails.

Discovered in 1996, Comet Hyakutake's tail was found to be over 550 million km (342 million miles) long – more than three times the distance between the Sun and Earth.

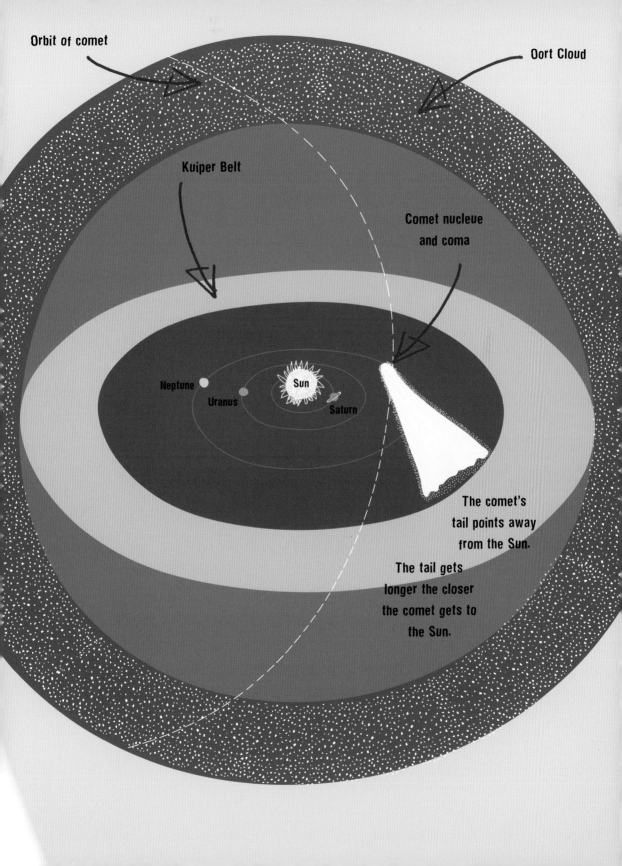

Orbit of comet

Oort Cloud

Kuiper Belt

Comet nucleue
and coma

Neptune

Uranus

Sun

Saturn

The comet's
tail points away
from the Sun.

The tail gets
longer the closer
the comet gets to
the Sun.

What else is out there?

Beyond the Solar System vast numbers of other stars lie in large groups called galaxies. Some galaxies are thought to contain billions of stars as well as planets and other mysterious bodies – such as black holes, from which no light can escape. There is great debate over whether Earth is the only place in the Universe where life flourishes. Does alien life exist somewhere out there?

Glossary

astronomer A scientist who studies the Sun, Moon, stars, planets and space in general.

black hole An area in space that nothing, not even light, can escape from, because **gravity** is so strong there.

dense Heavy in relation to its size, so that a tiny amount is extremely heavy.

element A simple chemical substance that is made up of atoms (the smallest part of an element) of only one type. It cannot be split into a simpler substance.

extraterrestrial Not from Earth.

event horizon The edge of the area around a **black hole**. Everything within the event horizon is sucked into the black hole.

exoplanet A planet in another planetary system.

galaxy A grouping of stars, dust and gas clouds that may also contain planets. Our galaxy is the **Milky Way**, which contains our Sun and its planets as well as many other stars. All the stars we can see without a telescope belong to the Milky Way.

gravity A force that pulls objects in space towards each other. Around Earth, it pulls them towards the planet, so things fall to the ground when you drop them.

light year The distance that light travels in one year.

Local Group The collection of galaxies that our **galaxy** is part of.

Milky Way Our home **galaxy**, a system of stars that contains a sun and planets.

orbit A curved path followed by a planet (or an object) as it moves around a planet or a star. To orbit is to go around another planet or star.

Solar System The Sun and all the planets and other objects that move around it.

supernova, Type II (plural supernovae) A star that suddenly becomes much brighter and gives out a huge amount of energy because it is exploding and will die.

telescope A scientific instrument that gathers in light or other signals from space to allow people to study distant objects.

Universe The whole of space and everything in it, including the Earth, the planets and the stars.

The Milky Way
...in 30 seconds

Earth's home galaxy is the Milky Way. It is a spiral galaxy that is between 100,000 and 120,000 light years wide and approximately 1,000 light years thick.

To give an idea of this size, if the Milky Way was shrunk to the size of a 100-metre (300-feet) football pitch, the whole Solar System would be a 2-mm (0.1-inch) grain of sand on it.

Just like the planets travel around the Sun, our Solar System travels around the centre of the Milky Way. It takes between 225 and 230 million years to complete an orbit.

The Milky Way is part of a cluster, or collection, of galaxies known as the Local Group. These include Andromeda, the Triangulam galaxy and Canis Major Dwarf as well as a further 40 galaxies, some of which have only recently been discovered. The Local Group has a diameter of about 10 million light years.

3-second sum-up

Our Sun is just one among 200 billion stars in the Milky Way.

3-minute mission Star count

Let's assume that there are 200 billion stars in the Milky Way – yes, that's 200,000,000,000! How many years would it take to count them all, assuming you can count a star every second? These tips should help you:

1 Use a calculator. Work out how many stars you could count in a day.

2 Multiply your day figure by 365.25 (to allow for the leap year every four years).

Answer on page 96

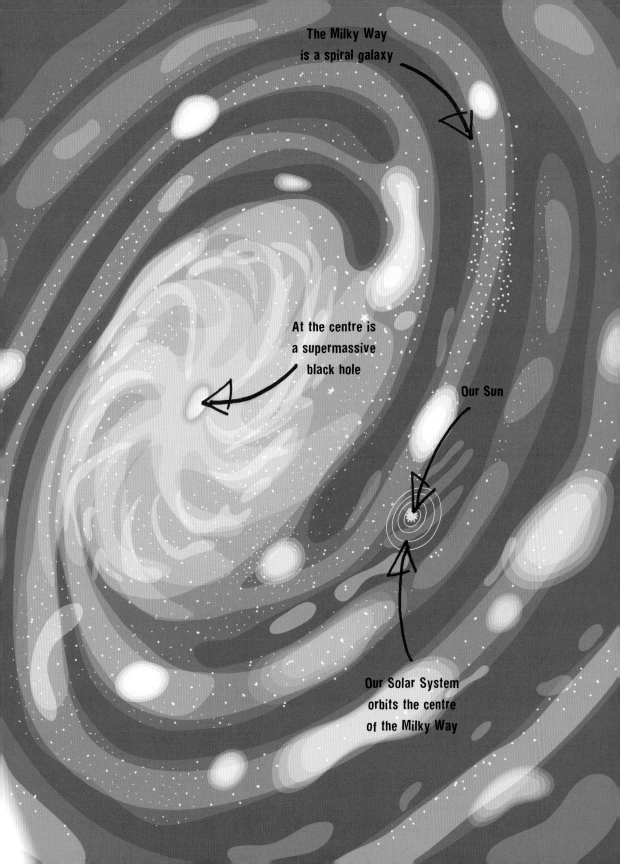

Galaxies

...in 30 seconds

The Universe contains large numbers of galaxies. Each is a vast collection of gas, dust, stars and planets. Most are impossible to spot from Earth because they are such huge distances away.

One of the Milky Way's nearest neighbours is the M31 Andromeda galaxy. Andromeda may be 220,000 light years across and contain as many as 800 billion stars.

Andromeda is moving towards the Milky Way at a rapid rate – over 140 km (87 miles) every second. Don't let this cause you sleepless nights though. Even at that speed, it will take over 3 billion years for the two galaxies to reach each other.

Astronomers place galaxies into broad groups based on their overall shape. The Milky Way and Andromeda are both spiral galaxies. Other galaxies are elliptical – oval-shaped – or round.

Lenticular galaxies are flat discs, often with a central bulge. Galaxies with no obvious shape are called irregular. They were probably pulled out of shape by gravity from other galaxies.

3-second sum-up

A galaxy is a vast collection of gas, dust, stars and planets.

3-minute mission Galaxy shapes

Go to NASA's images website – http://www.nasaimages.org – select Universe, and view a stunning selection of photos of distant galaxies.

1 Try to find two spiral galaxies besides Andromeda, the Whirlpool and the Milky Way.
2 Is the M87 galaxy irregular, elliptical or lenticular?
3 Is the M104 Sombrero galaxy irregular, spiral or elliptical?

Spiral galaxy

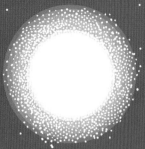

Elliptical galaxy

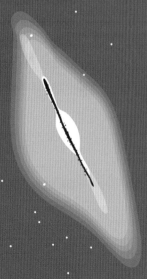

Lenticular galaxy

Irregular galaxy

Black holes

...in 30 seconds

No one has ever seen a black hole. It is a point in space where gravity is so strong that it pulls everything into it: all matter, gas, light – everything. A very dense mass in a tiny area generates this incredibly powerful gravity.

As far as we know, no object can ever escape from a black hole.

There is an area of space around a black hole from which light cannot escape. The very edge of this area is called the event horizon. Any energy or matter inside the event horizon cannot escape being drawn into the black hole's clutches.

Scientists believe that there are several types of black holes. Supermassive black holes are found in the centre of galaxies. Stellar black holes are formed after a supernova leaves behind a large, incredibly dense star core (centre). This large core keeps on collapsing in on itself, as the pull of gravity increases, until a black hole is formed.

How to see a black hole

If no light ever escapes from a black hole, how can we possibly see them? Excellent question.

Astronomers seek out black holes by measuring their effects on other bodies outside of them. For example, some black holes have been discovered by observing gas and dust from a star near a stellar black hole being pulled into them.

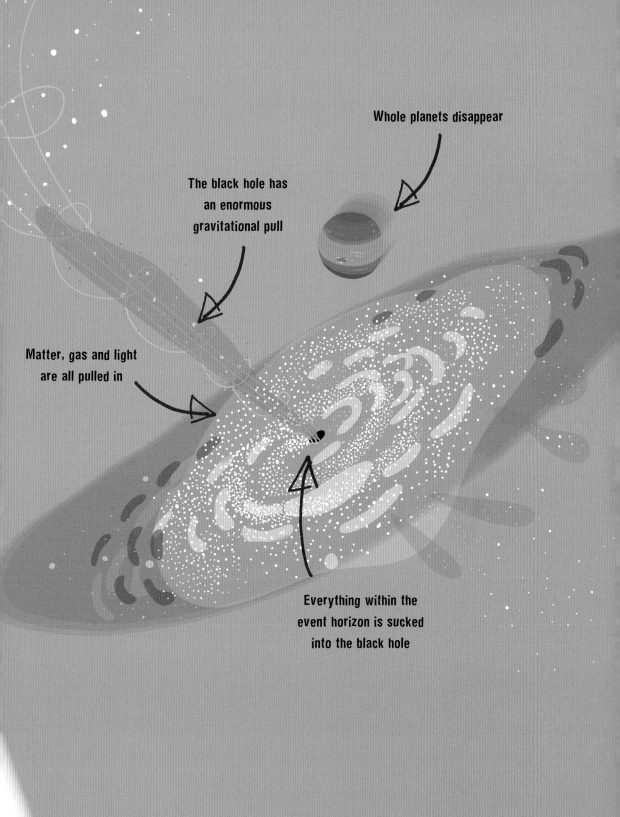

Whole planets disappear

The black hole has an enormous gravitational pull

Matter, gas and light are all pulled in

Everything within the event horizon is sucked into the black hole

Are there aliens?

...in 30 seconds

Does extraterrestrial life exist? No one knows for sure. Astronomers have scoured the Solar System and beyond without detecting any aliens. Yet the chemical elements that make up life on Earth are found throughout the Universe.

Given that the Universe is phenomenally huge, is it likely that a small planet in a single galaxy contains the Universe's only life?

The sheer scale of the Universe makes searching for aliens extremely hard. But some organizations scour radio telescope signals for signs of intelligent life. People have also tried to announce our presence to aliens. For example, radio signals that show key facts about Earth and humans have been beamed into space.

Some alien hunters are excited by the recent discovery of exoplanets – planets found orbiting stars other than the Sun. Over 700 have been found so far. Could any have the right conditions for life to form?

3-second sum-up

No aliens have been found . . . yet.

3-minute mission Contact aliens

Imagine you are designing an image to be beamed out into the Universe to make contact with alien life forms. What information would you include? How would you show it?

Aliens will not understand English! Think about symbols, signs and images that could show them humans, the Earth and its place in the Universe.

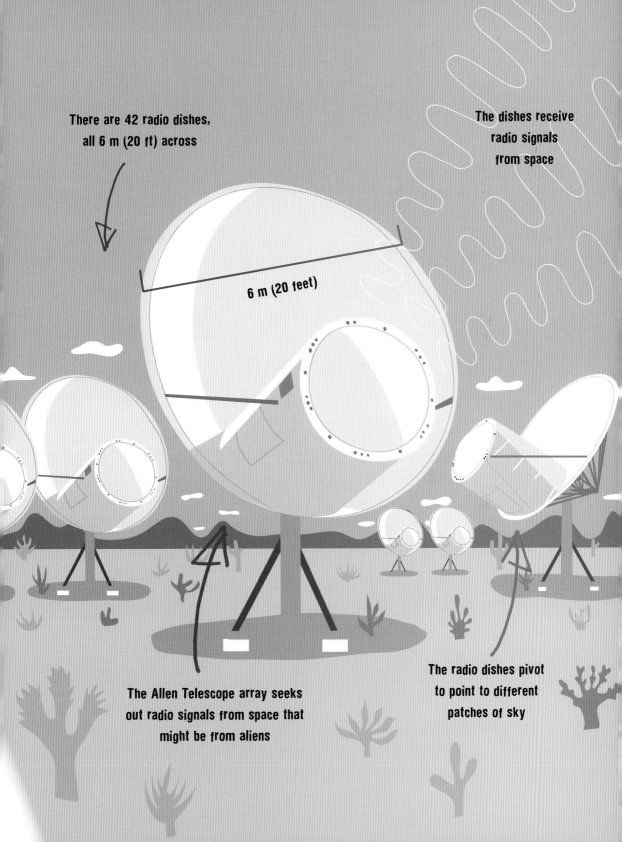

There are 42 radio dishes, all 6 m (20 ft) across

The dishes receive radio signals from space

6 m (20 feet)

The Allen Telescope array seeks out radio signals from space that might be from aliens

The radio dishes pivot to point to different patches of sky

Plotting the Universe

Before the telescope was invented, scientists knew little about the stars and planets. From the 16th century, scientists used telescopes to examine these bodies in more detail. Advances in the 20th century allowed humans, probes and scientific instruments to be carried into space for the first time. Now, telescopes and probes can send back amazingly detailed information about planets and moons across the Solar System.

Plotting the Universe
Glossary

amplifier Equipment that makes sounds or radio signals stronger and louder.

antenna (plural antennae) Equipment made of wire or long straight pieces of metal for receiving or sending radio signals.

aperture Opening.

astronomer A scientist who studies the Sun, Moon, stars, planets and space in general.

atmosphere The mixture of gases that surround a planet.

black hole An area in space that nothing can escape from, because **gravity** is so strong.

booster rocket The first stage of a rocket or additional rockets fitted to the main rocket. The booster rocket or rockets fire at launch time and drop away when their fuel is used up.

combustion A chemical reaction in which substances combine with oxygen to produce heat and light.

comet A mass of ice and dust that moves around the Sun.

exoplanet A planet in another planetary system.

galaxy A grouping of stars, dust and gas clouds that may also contain planets.

gravity A force that pulls objects in space towards each other. Around Earth, it pulls them towards the planet, so things fall to the ground when you drop them.

km/h Kilometres per hour; a measure of speed.

micrometeoroid A mini-meteoroid, a tiny piece of rock in space.

MMU A rocket-powered device that astronauts can wear so they can float freely in space.

mph Miles per hour; a measure of speed

nebula (plural nebulae) A huge cloud of dust and gas. Some nebulae form stars.

neutron star A type of extremely dense star.

optical telescope A telescope that gathers in light through its opening and makes objects in space appear much larger.

orbit A curved path followed by a planet or an object as it moves around a planet or star. To orbit is to go around a planet or star.

oxidizer A chemical that releases oxygen.

radio wave A type of electromagnetic wave with a long wavelength, used for communication on Earth and given off by a number of bodies in space.

reflecting telescope A form of **telescope** using smooth, curved mirrors to gather and focus light, to make images from space look bigger.

refracting telescope A kind of **telescope** with lenses to bend and focus light to make images from space look bigger.

satellite A device sent into space that moves around the Earth, Moon or another planet. It is used for communication, research and other tasks.

solar panel Equipment on space stations and some space probes that converts the Sun's light energy into electricity.

space probe A spacecraft without people on board that obtains information and sends it back to Earth.

supernova, Type II (plural supernovae) A star that suddenly becomes much brighter and gives out a huge amount of energy because it is exploding and dying.

telescope An instrument that gathers in light or other signals from space so people can study distant objects.

Universe The whole of space and everything in it, including the Earth, planets and stars.

weightlessness Having no weight. Occurs when there is no gravity.

Optical telescopes

...in 30 seconds

Optical telescopes gather in light from space through the aperture (opening). The first telescopes invented were refracting telescopes. They gather in far more light than a human eye. The light passes through a convex lens (it is thinner around the edges than in the centre). This bends the light so that it comes together and focuses at a point inside the telescope. A second lens in the telescope spreads the focused image out across your eye so the image is magnified.

Scientists found that bigger apertures and lenses could magnify objects more, but larger lenses were very heavy, hard to make and suffered from fringes of colour around their edges. A new form of telescope was developed using smooth, curved mirrors to gather and focus light. These reflecting telescopes can be astonishingly huge.

The Keck 1 and 2 telescopes on Hawaii each have mirrors made up of 36 separate segments that together have a diameter of 10 m (33 feet). These telescopes have amazing powers, able to spot objects millions of light years away. Scientists have used Keck telescopes to discover many exoplanets – planets orbiting distant stars.

3-second sum-up

Optical telescopes magnify distant objects in space.

3-minute mission Make a telescope

To make a simple telescope, find two plastic magnifying glass lenses, one bigger than the other. Hold one lens in each hand and place them in line, the bigger lens in front of the smaller.

Aim them at an object – a street light at dusk or night time is ideal – and look through them. Adjust the distance between the two lenses until your target object is nice and sharp.

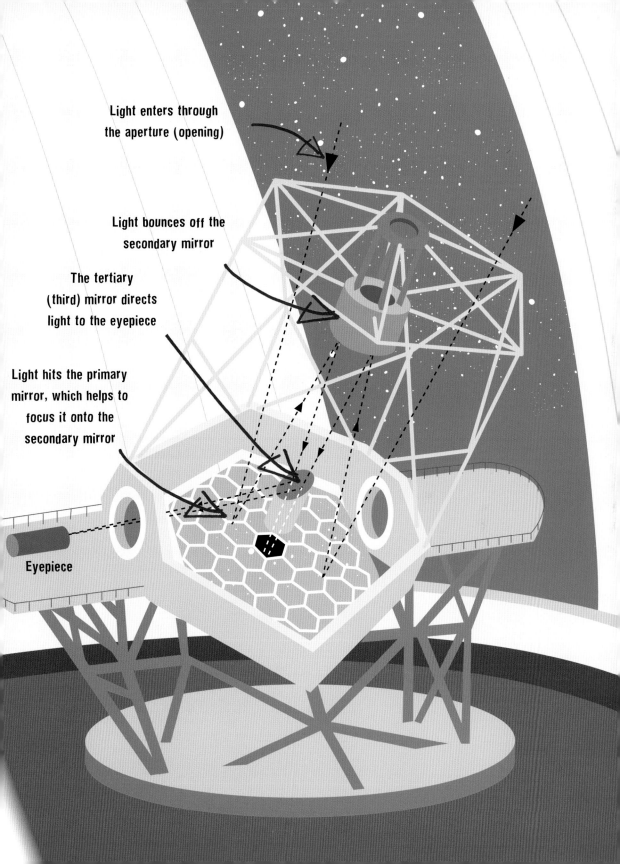

Light enters through the aperture (opening)

Light bounces off the secondary mirror

The tertiary (third) mirror directs light to the eyepiece

Light hits the primary mirror, which helps to focus it onto the secondary mirror

Eyepiece

Radio telescopes

...in 30 seconds

In the early 1930s, an American radio engineer, Karl Jansky, discovered radio signals coming from the Milky Way. Sounding like static or noise, they were given off by a radio source called Sagittarius A*, coming from what we now believe is a black hole. Other radio waves are given off by gases in space, by rotating neutron stars called pulsars and by some supernova remnants.

By studying the radio waves coming from these sources, astronomers can learn about the objects' structure, movement and what they are made from.

Radio astronomy is useful because it is not affected by daylight, clouds or rain. Radio waves can also travel through dust and can be used to study the hot, dusty nebulae in space.

Many radio telescopes use a series of small dishes linked together in an array.

3-second sum-up

Radio telescopes collect radio waves given off by objects in space.

Giant dishes

Some radio telescopes are single giant dishes. The Arecibo telescope in Puerto Rico has a dish that is a staggering 305 m (1,000 ft) in diameter.

By around 2016, it will be dwarfed by a new dish in China. Called FAST, it will be 500 m (1,640 ft) wide. Its dish area will be bigger than 25 football fields! FAST will be three times more sensitive than the Arecibo dish.

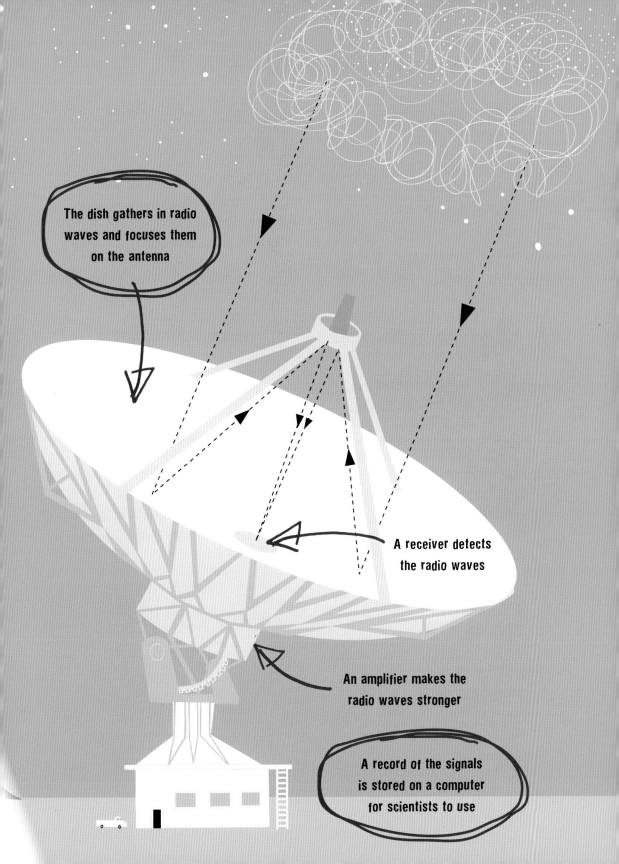

Space telescopes
...in 30 seconds

If you use an optical telescope on Earth, you have to peer through the Earth's atmosphere, which can absorb some waves and scatter light. Telescopes in space can produce sharp images of really distant parts of the Universe. They can work round the clock, not just at night as they can on Earth.

The Hubble Space Telescope (HST) was launched in 1990. It has taken more than 700,000 images of space and relayed them back to Earth. In 1994, it tracked a comet that crashed into Jupiter.

The Hubble has shown us things in the Universe we had never seen before. It helped to discover supermassive black holes and took images of exoplanets for the very first time.

One of Hubble's most famous photos is called the Hubble Ultra-Deep Field. Made from data gathered in 2003–04, it shows more than 10,000 galaxies, some as far back as 13 billion light years – less than a billion years after the Universe was formed.

3-second sum-up

Space telescopes show clear images of the Universe across space and time.

Snapshot in time

Light can take many millions or billions of years to travel from distant stars and galaxies to Earth.

This means that the view we get of a distant object is a history lesson. It shows the object as it was millions or billions of years earlier.

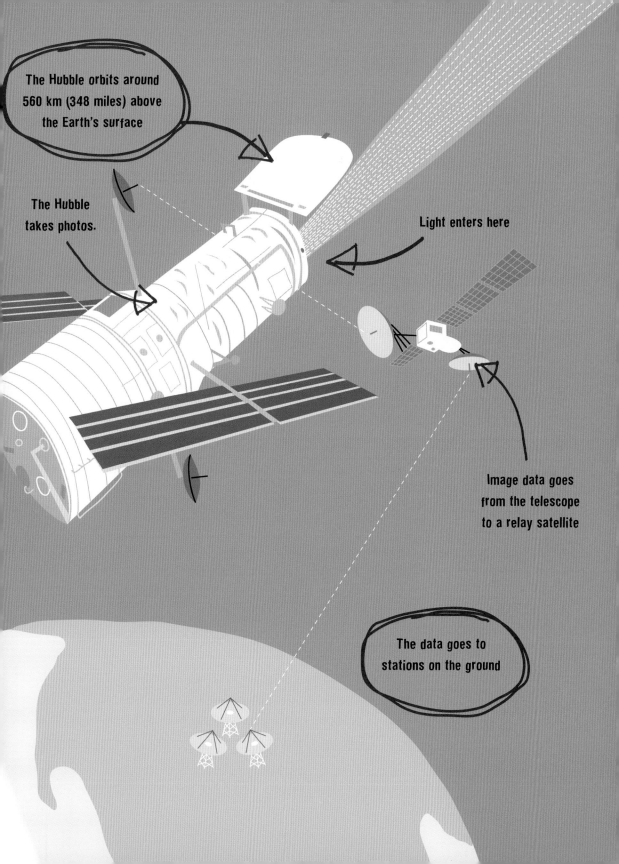

Rocket science

...in 30 seconds

Spacecraft need an enormous amount of power to lift off, overcome Earth's gravity and launch into space. A rocket is the launch vehicle.

In space, there is no oxygen to help fuel to burn. So rocket engines carry their own fuel and an oxygen-producing chemical called an oxidizer. The fuel and oxidizer are mixed together then burnt in large combustion chambers to produce huge amounts of gases. As these gases expand rapidly out of the exhausts of the engine downwards, the launch vehicle moves in the opposite direction, upwards.

Some launch vehicles use booster rockets. These fire at launch time and drop away as soon as their fuel is used up, removing weight from the launch vehicle. Other launch vehicles have two or three stages, each with their own rocket engine or engines. As each stage uses up its fuel, it falls away.

3-second sum-up

Rocket engines power launch vehicles and send them up into space.

3-minute mission Launch a rocket

1 Blow up a long balloon, fold over the open end and keep it shut with a clothes peg.

2 Run a long thread through a drinking straw. Tape the straw to the side of the balloon.

3 Tape the thread-end nearest the peg to the floor. Get a friend to hold up the other thread-end as high as possible. Push the balloon down and release the peg.

4 Lift off!

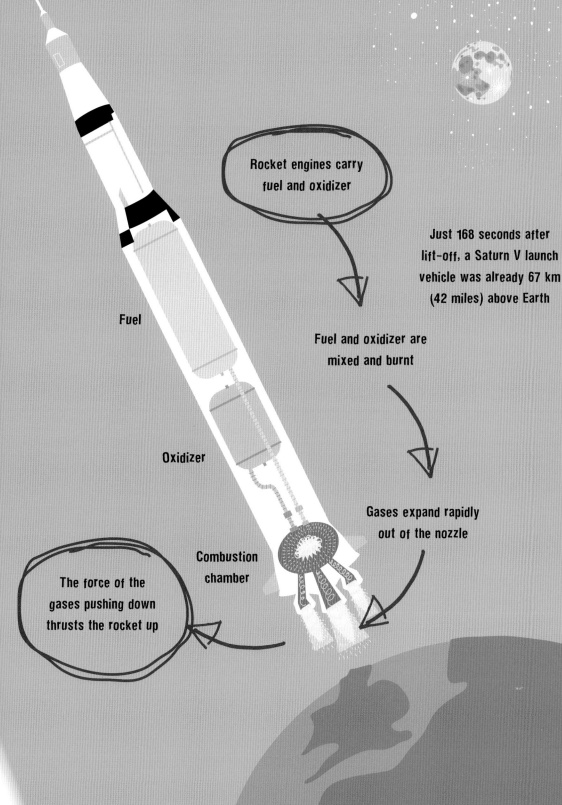

Space probes
...in 30 seconds

Some probes have orbited or landed on planets or their moons. Others have flown by asteroids or comets. They send vital information gathered by their scientific instruments back to Earth via radio waves that travel at the speed of light.

Space probes mostly go on one-way missions, never to return to Earth. Without precious humans on board, some travel to hostile places sending back data until they're destroyed.

A handful of probes do return. Part of the Stardust probe came back in 2006 after its 1999 launch, with dust samples from the tail of the comet Wild 2.

The Mars Exploration Rover B (MER-B) was extraordinarily successful. After landing on Mars in January 2004, its mission was supposed to last 90 Martian days. The six-wheeled, solar-powered rover managed to work for more than 30 times longer!

3-second sum-up

Space probes explore the Solar System.

3-minute mission Space probe quiz

Go to the Cassini space probe webpage: http://saturn.jpl.nasa.gov/mission/quickfacts and answer these questions:

1 The Huygens probe landed on a Saturn moon that had the same name as the rocket that launched Cassini. Which was it?

2 How many Cassini probes equal the weight of its launch vehicle, a Titan rocket?

3 How many days from its launch did Cassini take to arrive at Saturn? Don't forget leap years!

Answer on page 96

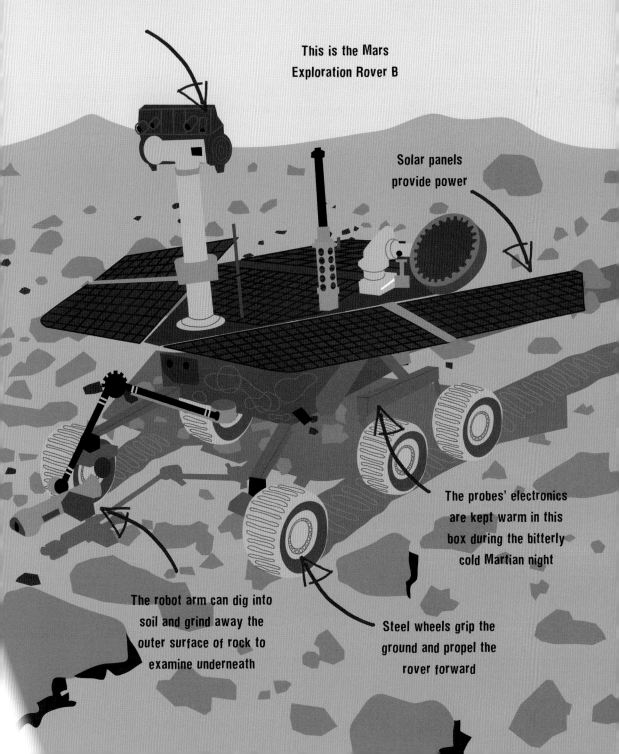

The cameras allow the rover to
find its way around Mars

This is the Mars
Exploration Rover B

Solar panels
provide power

The probes' electronics
are kept warm in this
box during the bitterly
cold Martian night

The robot arm can dig into
soil and grind away the
outer surface of rock to
examine underneath

Steel wheels grip the
ground and propel the
rover forward

Weightlessness

...in 30 seconds

Some astronauts spend long periods of time on spacecraft such as the International Space Station.

Life in space poses special challenges for the human body. On Earth, gravity presses down on your skeleton, but when orbiting in space, astronauts experience weightlessness.

The weightlessness is because the spacecraft is falling through space. The discs between the bones of astronauts' spines expand a little, and they grow slightly taller!

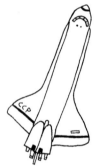

Inside a spacecraft, you can't eat normally. Food crumbs would float away, fouling up instruments and making a terrible mess. Astronauts eat specially designed food. They have high-tech toilets, with air to flush away waste. Astronauts shower in a sealed shower pod and afterwards, air sucks away the water droplets.

3-second sum-up

In space, humans experience weightlessness.

3-minute mission **Match the milestones**

Match the astronauts (right) to their space milestones (left).

First person in space, 1961	**John Glenn**
First woman in space, 1963	**Susan J. Helms and James S. Voss**
Most time in space	
First spacewalk, 1965	**Sergei Krikalev**
Longest single spacewalk: 8 hours, 56 minutes, 2001	**Valentina Tereshkova**
	Yuri Gargarin
Oldest astronaut: 77 years, 1998	**Alexei Leonov**

Answer on page 96

Spacesuits
...in 30 seconds

Space is a hostile place for humans. Tiny particles called micrometeoroids can whizz by at speeds fast enough to rip through flesh. There's no air to breathe. You get extremely hot in the sunlight and freezing cold in shadow.

Modern spacecraft contain air so astronauts can wear normal clothes. For lift-off from Earth and trips outside the spacecraft, they wear spacesuits.

First, the astronaut puts on a maximum absorption garment (an adult nappy) because there are no toilets out in space! He or she also puts on special water-cooled underwear. Next is an electrical harness that contains all the circuits and wiring for the radio and devices that monitor the astronaut's health.

The main suit is white to reflect the Sun's heat energy. It is thick to stop injury from particles whizzing by. The suit is linked to a backpack, the Primary Life Support System (PLSS). This controls the temperature inside the suit and provides oxygen and electricity for the suit's electrical parts.

3-second sum-up

A spacesuit is a complete life-support system for an astronaut.

Spacewalks

Astronauts go on extravehicular activities (EVAs), or spacewalks, to do space experiments, capture a satellite or to check or repair a spacecraft.

The astronaut is usually connected to the outside of the spacecraft by a tether. But the MMU, a rocket-powered device used in 1984, allowed astronauts to fly freely in space.

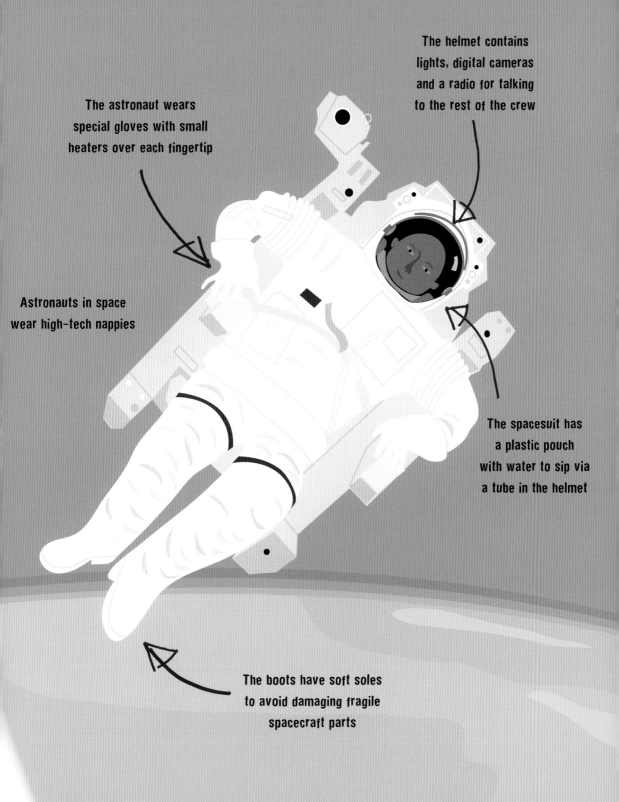

The helmet contains lights, digital cameras and a radio for talking to the rest of the crew

The astronaut wears special gloves with small heaters over each fingertip

Astronauts in space wear high-tech nappies

The spacesuit has a plastic pouch with water to sip via a tube in the helmet

The boots have soft soles to avoid damaging fragile spacecraft parts

International Space Station

...in 30 seconds

The International Space Station (ISS) is the largest space station to be launched. It is four times bigger than the Russian Mir space station launched in 1986. Since 1998, 100 missions from Earth have built it up, module by module.

Giant solar array wings (SAWs) provide electrical power for the ISS. Each wing has an area of over 300 square metres (2,200 square feet) and has 32,800 solar cells to convert the Sun's energy into electricity.

Inside the ISS are crew quarters, places for visiting spacecraft to dock, two bathrooms, an exercise gym and plenty of working areas as well as storage places for tools, supplies and experiments.

Hundreds of different science experiments are performed on the ISS. Some are about the effects of weightlessness on materials and creatures while others are to examine the Earth below or to learn more about humans in space.

3-second sum-up

A space station the size of a football pitch orbits 400 km (250 miles) above Earth.

ISS – the stats

Built by: the USA, Russia, Japan, Canada, and the European Space Agency

Length: 74 m (240 ft)

Width: 110 m (36 ft)

Orbital speed: Around 27,700 km/h (17,200 mph)

Expeditions: 31 (by 2012)

Distance travelled: Over 2.8 million km (1.7 million miles)

First crew: Expedition 1 (2000) spent 136 days on board

Operational life: up to 2020 or 2028

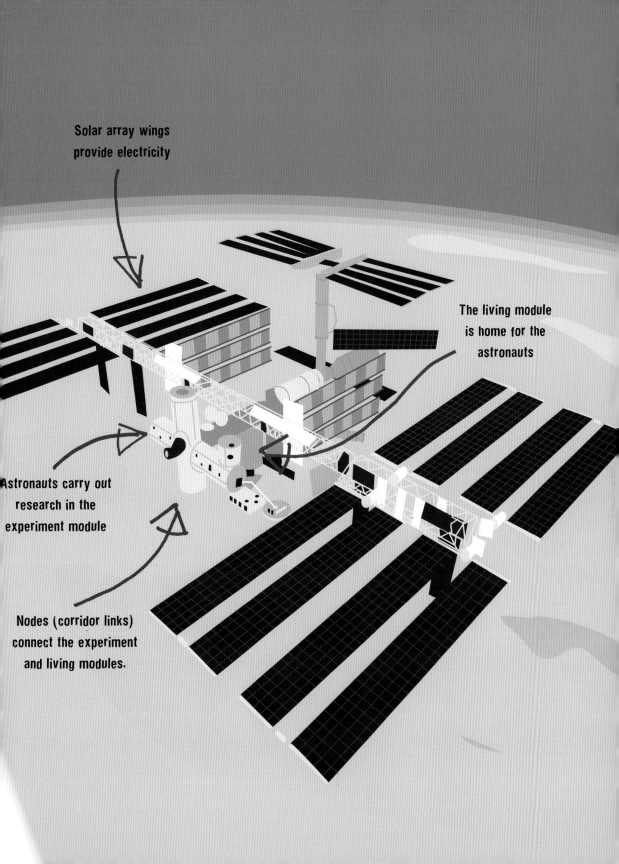

Solar array wings provide electricity

The living module is home for the astronauts

Astronauts carry out research in the experiment module

Nodes (corridor links) connect the experiment and living modules.

Discover more

NON-FICTION BOOKS

13 Planets: The Latest View of the Solar System by David A. Aguilar
National Geographic Society, 2011

Black Holes by Ker Than
Children's Press, 2010

Book of Astronomy and Space by Lisa Miles and Alastair Smith
Usborne, 2009

The Comic Strip History of Space by Tracey Turner
Bloomsbury, 2009

First Encyclopedia of Space by Paul Dowsell
Usborne, 2010

The Everything Kids Astronomy Book by Kathi Wagner
Adams, 2008

Out of this World: All the Cool bits about Space by Clive Gifford
Buster Books, 2011

The Pop Up, Pull Out Space Book
Dorling Kindersley, 2010

Science: Sorted! Space, Black Holes and Stuff by Glenn Murphy
Macmillan Children's Books, 2010

See Inside Space (See Inside):
With over 50 flaps to lift & a little book of Star Maps by Katie Daynes
Usborne, 2008

Space: A Children's Encyclopedia
Dorling Kindersley, 2010

Spacecraft and the Journey into Space by Raman Prinja
QED Publishing, 2012

DVDs – suitable for all ages

Discovery Channel – NASA's Greatest Missions Go Entertain, 2009

Earth and Space History Channel, 2011

Wonders of the Solar System, starring Brian Cox
2entertain, 2010

WEBSITES

Amazing Space
http://amazing-space.stsci.edu
All about the universe, using Hubble Space Telescope's discoveries

Esa Kids
www.esa.int/esaKIDSen/
European Space Agency site about our universe and life in space

Eyes on the Solar System
http://eyes.nasa.gov/index.html
A site full of real NASA mission data

Kids Astronomy
www.kidsastronomy.com
Information about space and exploration, and games

Mars Exploration Program
http://marsprogram.jpl.nasa.gov/participate/funzone/
All about Mars and missions to Mars, with games

The Space Place
http://spaceplace.nasa.gov
Facts, activities and games from NASA

Index

Quiz answers

page 64: star count

Answer: 60 x 60 x 24 = 86,400 stars counted per day
86,400 x 365.25 = 31,557,600 stars counted per year
Divide 200,000,000,000 by 31,557,600 = 6,337.62 years!

page 84: space probe quiz

1. Titan
2. 175
3. 15 October 1997 to 30 June 2004. Days (including leap years and 30 June 2004) = 2,451, which is 6 years, 8 months and 16 days.

page 86: match the milestones

First person in space, 1961:
Yuri Gargarin

First woman in space, 1963:
Valentina Tereshkova

Most time in space: 803 days over six different missions (1988–2005):
Sergei Krikalev

First spacewalk (Extravehicular Activity or EVA), 1965:
Alexei Leonov

Longest single spacewalk – 8 hours, 56 minutes, 2001:
Susan J. Helms and James S. Voss

Oldest ever astronaut – 77 years of age (1998):
John Glenn